VINCENZO PAOLILLO

SEYCHELLES

*To Sandra, whose impatience with little things
is only matched by her patience with big ones.*

*To the friends who have shared some exciting
times, especially Alberto and Gianfranco.*

SWAN·HILL
PRESS

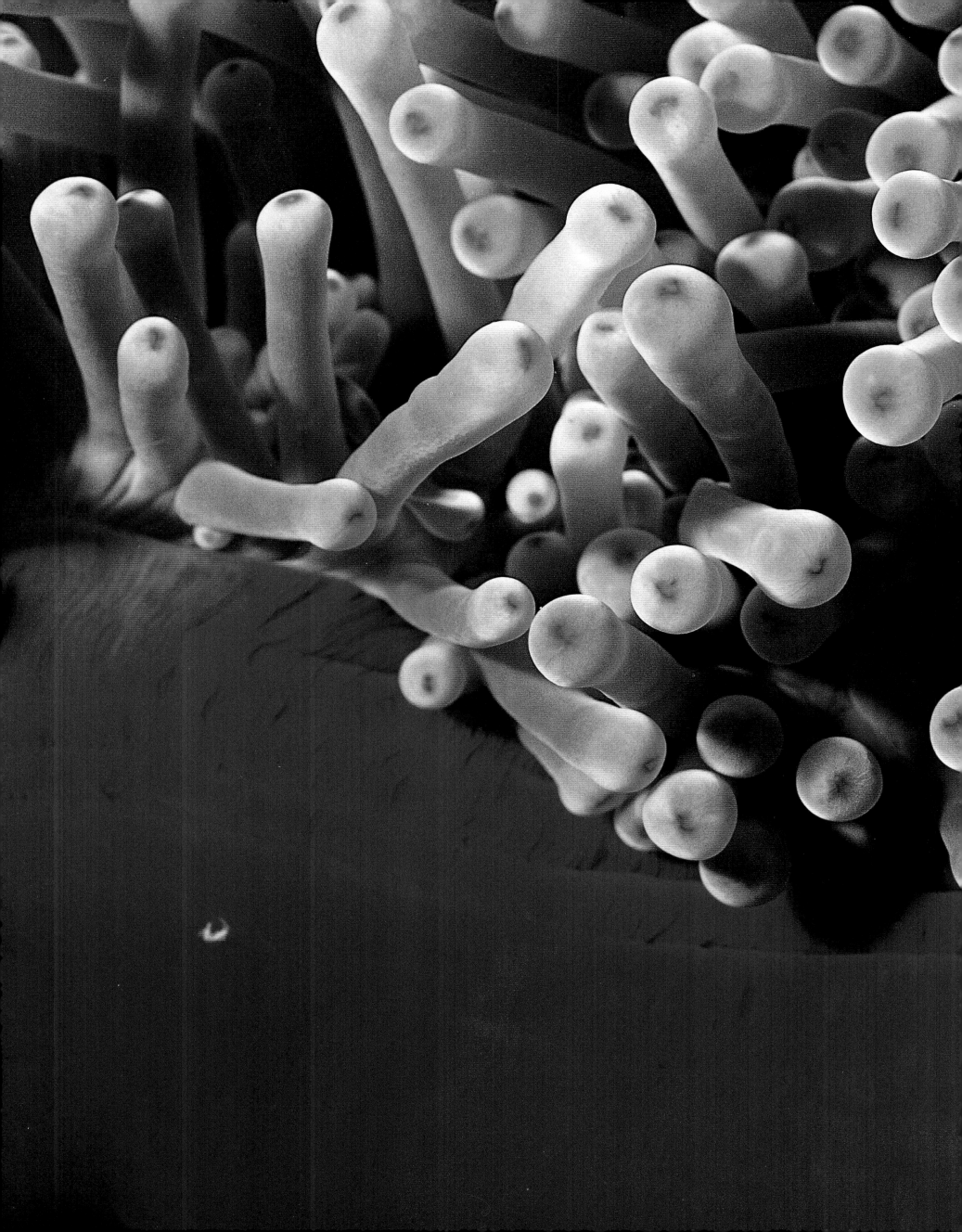

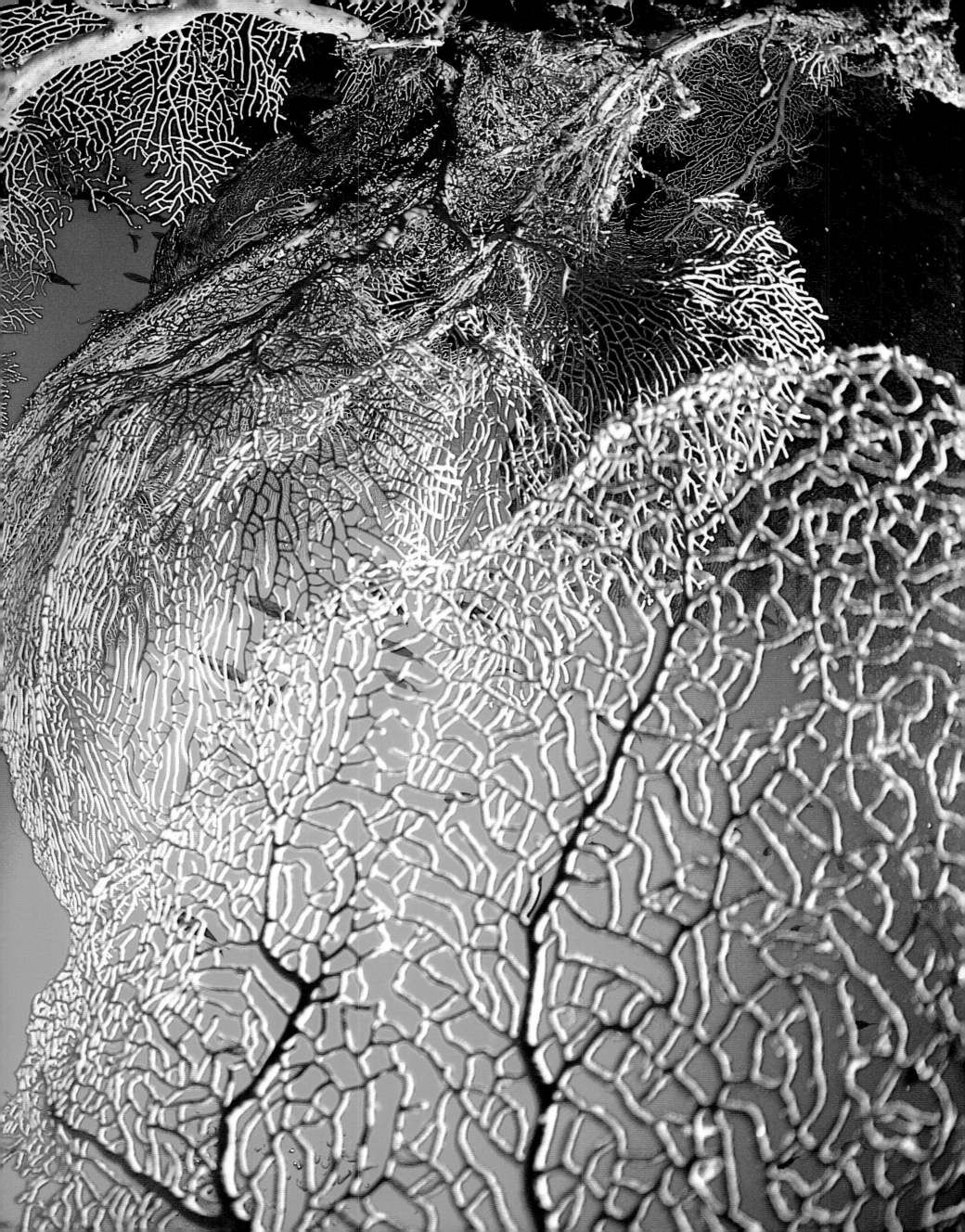

SEYCHELLES

Text and photographs
Vincenzo Paolillo

Scientific advisor
Angelo Mojetta

Editorial Production
Valeria Manferto De Fabianis

Graphic Design
Anna Galliani

Translation by
A.B.A.

CONTENTS

The author wishes to thank the Tourism Board of the Seychelles Ministry of Tourism and Transport, Howard Rosenstein, the Fantasea *crew, Betty Almogy and Patrick Bijou.*

1 The sun illuminates the great fans of gorgonians projecting from the vertical walls of Astove.

2-3 The silver pompano *(Trachinotus blochii)* is definitely one of the most magnificent fish living in the waters of Aldabra and Astove.

4-5 The pink "comma" decorating the tip of its tentacles perfectly matches the coat of this sea anemone *(Heteractis magnifica)*.

6-7 Attractive sea fans of the species *Subergorgia hicksoni* are a common sight just a few metres below the surface at Aldabra.

8-9 Potato cod *(Epinephelus tukula)*, which grow to over 1.5 metres long, are regular diving companions in the waters of Aldabra.

10-11 Dense shoals of big-eye trevally *(Caranx sexfasciatus)* are hunting on the sandy plateaux of Aldabra and Astove.

12-13 A multitude of coral-dwelling fish of various species swim among the mangrove branches in the Aldabra lagoon. These are inkwell snappers *(Lutjanus ehrenbergii)*, so called because of the black spot on the side.

© 1997 White Star S.r.l.
Via Candido Sassone, 22/24
13100 Vercelli, Italy.

First Published in the UK in 1997 by Swan Hill Press, an imprint of Airlife Publishing Ltd.

British Library
Cataloguing in Publication Data
A catalogue record for this book is available from the British Library

ISBN: 1 85310 937 1

Printed in the month of March 1997 by Pozzo Gros Mont, Turin. Colour separation Fotolito Garbero, Turin (Italy).

SWAN HILL PRESS
an imprint of Airlife Publishing Ltd.
101 Longden Road,
Shrewsbury SY3 9EB, England

INTRODUCTION

Two hundred and fifty million years ago, at the end of the Primary Era, two great continents constituted all the dry land on the earth's surface: Laurasia, which covered the northern hemisphere, and from which North America, Europe and Asia derived, and Gondwanaland, which covered the southern hemisphere.

Shortly afterwards (relatively speaking), at the beginning of the Secondary Era, Gondwanaland began to break up: the Antarctic-Australia block drifted east, while India drifted north to join up with Laurasia.

All that remained between them was Madagascar and a relatively small mass, mainly underwater; however, a few peaks emerged from the sea which were to appear on Portuguese navigators' charts millions of years later with the name of the "Seven Sisters" or "Seven Brothers", and were eventually called the Seychelles after the Finance Minister of Louis XV of France.

The islands, made of granite over six hundred and fifty million years old, rest on a large plateau just under sea level, and some rise to nearly 1,000 metres high.

The Seychelles are ancient in geological terms, but have only been inhabited since relatively recent times. Although the first traces of the islands date back to 16th-century Portuguese

14 top The clouds reflect the green of the surrounding land onto the waters of Aldabra lagoon; the East Channel can be seen beneath them.

14 centre The *Fantasea*, the comfortable boat that took around the waters of the Seychelles sea and Aldabra, rides the crystal-clear waves of the Indian Ocean.

14 bottom Alphonse is a marvellous coral island, situated halfway between Mahé and the Aldabra Group.

14-15 From the plane, Aldabra suddenly appears in the middle of the ocean, three hours' flying time from Mahé.

15 bottom left The largest area and height above sea level (18 metres) of the dry land at Aldabra is found towards Hodoul Point. Bras Takamaka, the furthermost promontory of the lagoon, can be seen in the left foreground.

15 bottom right Mangroves reign supreme in the inner lagoon of Aldabra, creating the ideal habitat for numerous species of fish.

16 top Apart from frigate birds, red-footed boobies form the largest colonies of sea birds in the islands of the Aldabra Group; there are white *(Sula sula)*, masked *(Sula dactylatra)* and brown *(Sula leucogaster)* species.

maps, they were certainly not discovered by a Portuguese caravel but by an Indonesian canoe or perhaps an Arab dhow from the Maldives. The latter hypothesis is supported by the legend (certainly pre-16th century) of the *coco de mer*, the famous sea coconut that only grows here, which weighs up to 40 kilograms and has the disturbing shape of a woman's pelvis, with a prominent mount of Venus. The coconut does not float, so it can hardly have been carried along by the waves to the Maldives as the legend has it; it is more likely that a sailor found it in the Seychelles and kept the secret of its discovery, telling this story to conceal its origin.

The first definite reports of the islands date from the early 16th century, when Vasco da Gama is said to have passed by them during one of his voyages from the Cape of Good Hope to India (in fact the Amirantes, another group of islands situated on the underwater ridge that stretches from Mauritius to Mahé, which have always been part of the Seychelles, are named after him).

The first report of a visit dates from a century later when, in 1609, a ship from the English East India company, the *Ascension*, came in sight of Mahé. The men who went ashore found crocodiles, turtles, coconuts, all kinds of birds and lush vegetation.

16 bottom Over 150,000 giant tortoises *(Geochelone gigantea)* live on Aldabra. The largest specimens grow to 40-50 kilos, while those in captivity can weigh as much as 150 kilos.

16-17 The islands of Cosmoledo offer a particularly suitable nesting area for the booby. Each bird lays and hatches a single egg, sometimes in the mangrove branches and sometimes on the ground.

17 bottom left The fluffy white booby chicks spend the first part of their lives in the mangrove branches.

17 bottom right A red-footed booby shows off its flying skills. The name derives from the Spanish *bobo*, which means clown.

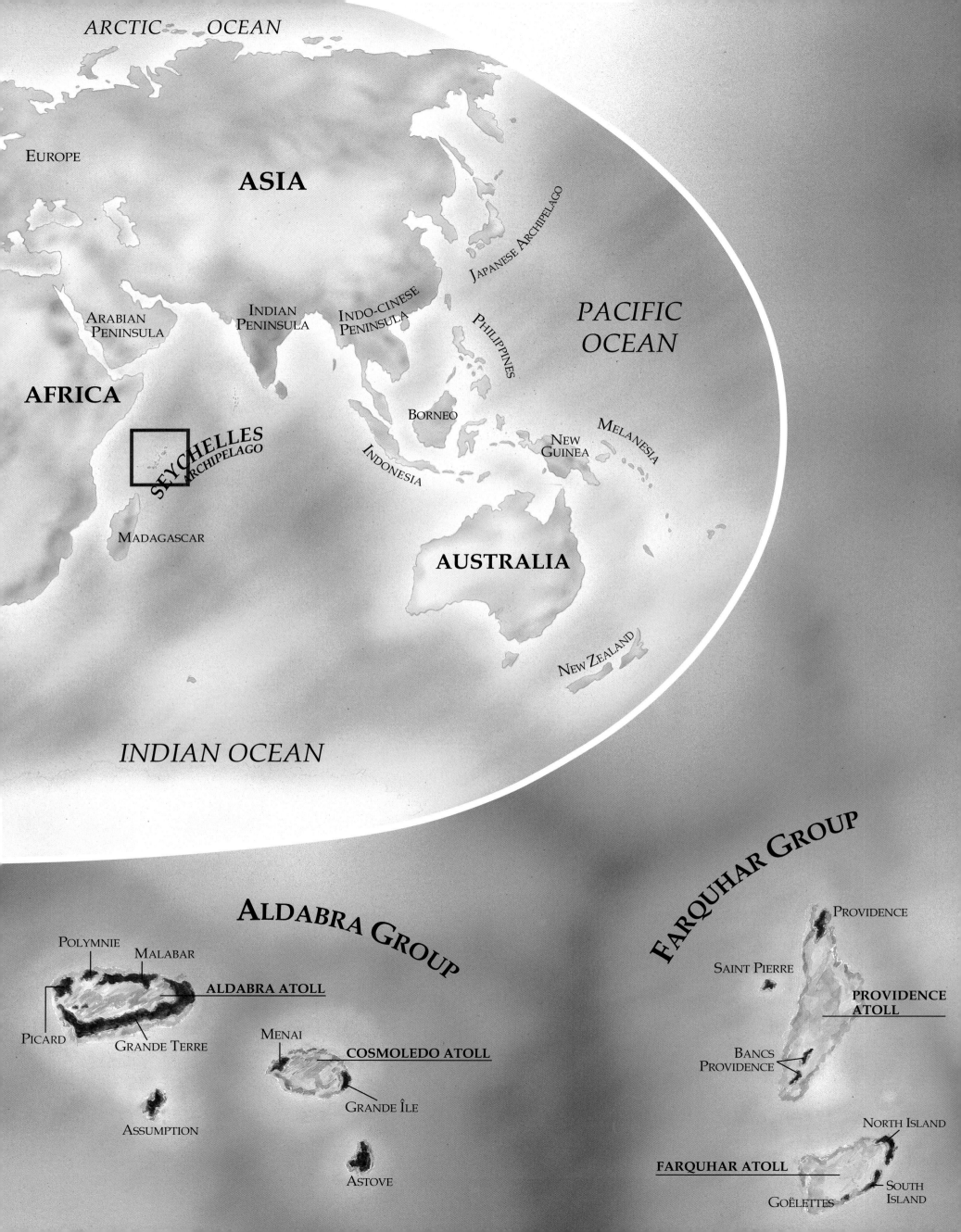

ARCTIC OCEAN

EUROPE

ASIA

PACIFIC OCEAN

ARABIAN PENINSULA

INDIAN PENINSULA

INDO-CINESE PENINSULA

JAPANESE ARCHIPELAGO

PHILIPPINES

AFRICA

SEYCHELLES ARCHIPELAGO

BORNEO

INDONESIA

NEW GUINEA

MELANESIA

MADAGASCAR

AUSTRALIA

NEW ZEALAND

INDIAN OCEAN

ALDABRA GROUP

FARQUHAR GROUP

POLYMNIE

MALABAR

PICARD

GRANDE TERRE

ALDABRA ATOLL

ASSUMPTION

MENAI

COSMOLEDO ATOLL

GRANDE ÎLE

ASTOVE

PROVIDENCE

SAINT PIERRE

PROVIDENCE ATOLL

BANCS PROVIDENCE

NORTH ISLAND

FARQUHAR ATOLL

GOËLETTES

SOUTH ISLAND

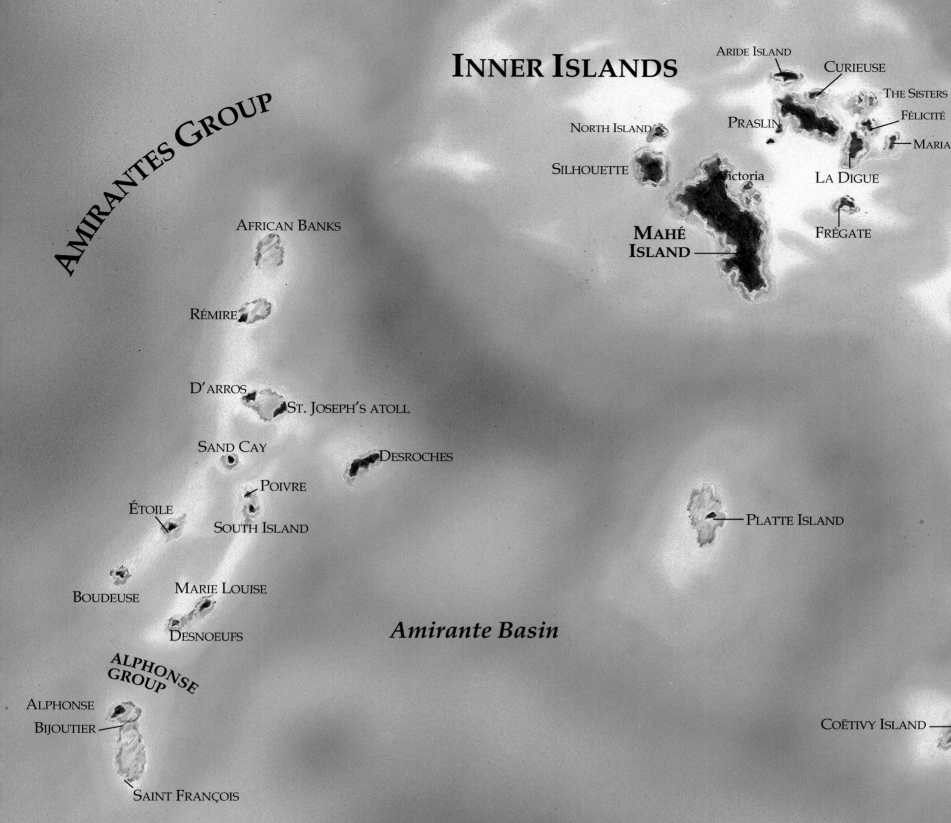

BIRD ISLAND

DENIS ISLAND

INNER ISLANDS

ARIDE ISLAND

CURIEUSE

THE SISTERS

FÉLICITÉ

PRASLIN

NORTH ISLAND

MARIANNE

SILHOUETTE

La Digue

Victoria

MAHÉ ISLAND

FRÉGATE

AMIRANTES GROUP

AFRICAN BANKS

RÉMIRE

D'ARROS

ST. JOSEPH'S ATOLL

SAND CAY

DESROCHES

POIVRE

ÉTOILE

SOUTH ISLAND

PLATTE ISLAND

BOUDEUSE

MARIE LOUISE

DESNOEUFS

Amirante Basin

ALPHONSE GROUP

ALPHONSE

BIJOUTIER

COËTIVY ISLAND

SAINT FRANÇOIS

Amirante Trench

INDIAN OCEAN

In later years the islands probably constituted the refuge, hiding place and supply base for pirates who had moved from the Caribbean to the Indian Ocean to attack merchant vessels en route to India, hence the many legends of buried treasure, which is still being sought today.

Apart from these occasional visits, the islands remained uninhabited. It was not until the mid-18th century that the idea of a permanent settlement was first considered. The Governor of Mauritius, Mahé de la Bourdonnais (after whom Mahé, the largest island in the archipelago, was named) sent the first sailing ships to establish the feasibility of his project, which was only to be carried out some years later by his successor, for military reasons. The Seven Years' War between France and England had broken out, and the archipelago acquired great strategic importance on the route to the Indies. On 1st November 1756 a French expedition officially took possession of the island of Mahé with a handful of French colonists and African slaves.

Henceforth, the history of the Seychelles was influenced by the wars between France and England. It again became the base for pirates, who openly backed the French. Some particularly celebrated pirates were Surcouf, the gallant pirate and Hodoul, after whom the

20-21 Various types of gorgonian sea fans grow on the walls of Alphonse, and numerous coral-dwelling fish, especially damselfish and anthias, play among their branches. The light that manages to filter through from the surface creates some attractive effects, enhancing the delicate beauty of the great sea fans.

East Point of Aldabra is named; the inscription *il fut juste* (he was fair) appears on his tomb in the old cemetery of Mahé. However, this triggered a reaction by the English, who occupied the islands on several occasions until they permanently took possession of them in 1811 after conquering all the most important strategic points in the Indian Ocean.

British rule (direct or indirect) lasted for over one hundred and sixty years, until the archipelago was granted its independence in 1976. French rule lasted just over forty years, yet oddly enough, French civilisation, customs and culture were at least as influential as their English counterparts. French and English are the official languages, and Creole, a French-based dialect dating back to the time of slavery, is also spoken. 80% of the population are Catholic, and there is a small Protestant minority. Many of the place names are French, the songs and dances possess many features of French origin, and the old houses are designed in the typical French colonial style.

The population is made up of an incredible mixture of races: the first French colonists, accompanied by slaves of African descent, were joined by Creoles of African and French descent, slaves freed from Arab slave traders by the English navy, and later by Indians, Indonesians, Madagascans and Chinese.

The various races did not remain separate, but intermarried, often with very strange but attractive results.

The Amirantes Group, the Alphonse Archipelago, the Farquhar Islands and the Aldabra Group, which are known as the outer islands and became part of the Seychelles Republic at different periods (the Aldabra Group was the last), have a very different structure from the inner islands. They occupy a total marine area of around 1.3 million square kilometres, only a small part of which is covered by dry land, stretching as far as 10° latitude south, close to the African coast and the great island of Madagascar.

They are all of coral origin; some are small islands, with an area of no more than a few square kilometres, little more than tiny patches of sand one or two metres high which become much smaller at high tide. These green gems in the blue sea are of far more recent origin than the inner islands. Others are atolls, some of them quite extensive, which grow on a basalt base of volcanic origin rising from the depths of the sea.

The largest of all is Aldabra atoll, which has also been studied most because of its special features. It is the result of four successive sedimentations of calcium carbonate, the material of which all atolls are formed, after the

22-23 Encounters with turtles are quite common during dives in the waters of Aldabra, Astove and Assumption. Divers will usually see the green turtle *(Chelonia mydas)*, but the loggerhead *(Caretta caretta)* and the hawksbill turtle *(Eretmochelys imbricata)* shown here are also quite common.

24-25 Cousin Island, situated some 3 kilometres off Praslin Island, has been a member of the International Council for the Protection of Birds since 1968. During the nesting period, between April and May, the island plays host to some 250,000 birds of various species.

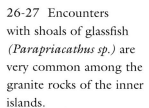

26-27 Encounters with shoals of glassfish (*Parapriacathus sp.*) are very common among the granite rocks of the inner islands.

land has repeatedly emerged above and sunk below sea level. This phenomenon took place between one and two million years ago, and is thus far more recent than the origin of the inner islands.

Even to the least expert eye the dry land clearly shows evidence of two successive sedimentations, one at 4 metres and one at 8 metres above sea level; it consists of a succession of coral rocks, in the middle of which rough, eroded, pockmarked fossils of coral can be clearly seen, interrupted by holes, grottoes and tunnels penetrating below the surface, resulting from the action of wind and rain.

The outer islands are mainly uninhabited or sparsely populated; in some cases they are linked to Mahé by small airfields built in recent years, but most can only be reached by sea. The sea is obviously the dominant element; it influences human, animal, vegetable and mineral life, determines the climate and supplies the main source of sustenance.

For centuries, the islands' inhabitants mainly ate fish; nowadays, tuna fishing and conservation, together with tourism, constitute the main resource of the country's economy.

The Seychelles are situated in the middle of the Indian Ocean, over 1,500 kilometres from the African coast (only the Aldabra group comes much closer to the continent and other large land masses), where the ocean depths are interrupted by great shelves, platforms that rise nearly to the surface; there is a continual turnover of water, and the sea is still teeming with life and so far pollution-free.

This is rightly considered one of the best deep-sea fishing areas in the world, and is very popular with fishermen looking for record catches. Above all the variety of situations, environments and habitats make this one of the healthiest and richest seas in the world, and the largest number of organisms, fish,

corals and specimens of all the life forms existing in the Indian Ocean is to be found here.

The environment is extremely varied. The inner islands, made of granite, stand on an underwater plateau no more than 50-60 metres down; coral clings to the rock, which is penetrated by grottoes, holes and ravines, providing the ideal habitat for all kinds of creatures – coral-feeding species, predators, fish that like swimming in the open and those which prefer dark lairs. Some of the outer islands have a mainly coralline structure, and rise suddenly from awesome depths, such as Poivre, the Farquhar Atoll and above all Astove, with its seemingly bottomless drop-offs, which are difficult for divers and often tormented by strong currents, but offer a wealth of encounters and surprises. The Aldabra atoll is also made of coral, but is gentler; here, open areas are followed by quiet coves, and finally the incredible inner lagoon, where snorkelling among the mangroves is no less exciting than diving deep down in the open sea.

The common characteristic is the great variety of life forms encountered on every dive, from the tiniest to the most awe-inspiring.

Researchers have an abundance of choice, and divers can take their pick of exciting, different experiences, some of them absolutely unique and incomparable.

24 bottom left A young sea swallow (*Phaeton lepturus*), one of the small but attractive tropical birds that can be found on some of the inner islands of the Seychelles, timidly poses for the cameraman.

24 bottom right This photo shows a fairy tern chick; the fairy tern (*Gygis alba*) is the bird with the white coat and blue beak chosen by *Air Seychelles* as its symbol.

25 Huge granite rocks, oddly shaped by the action of the wind and waves, are scattered over the beaches of Curieuse, a small island near Praslin, on which giant turtles are raised.

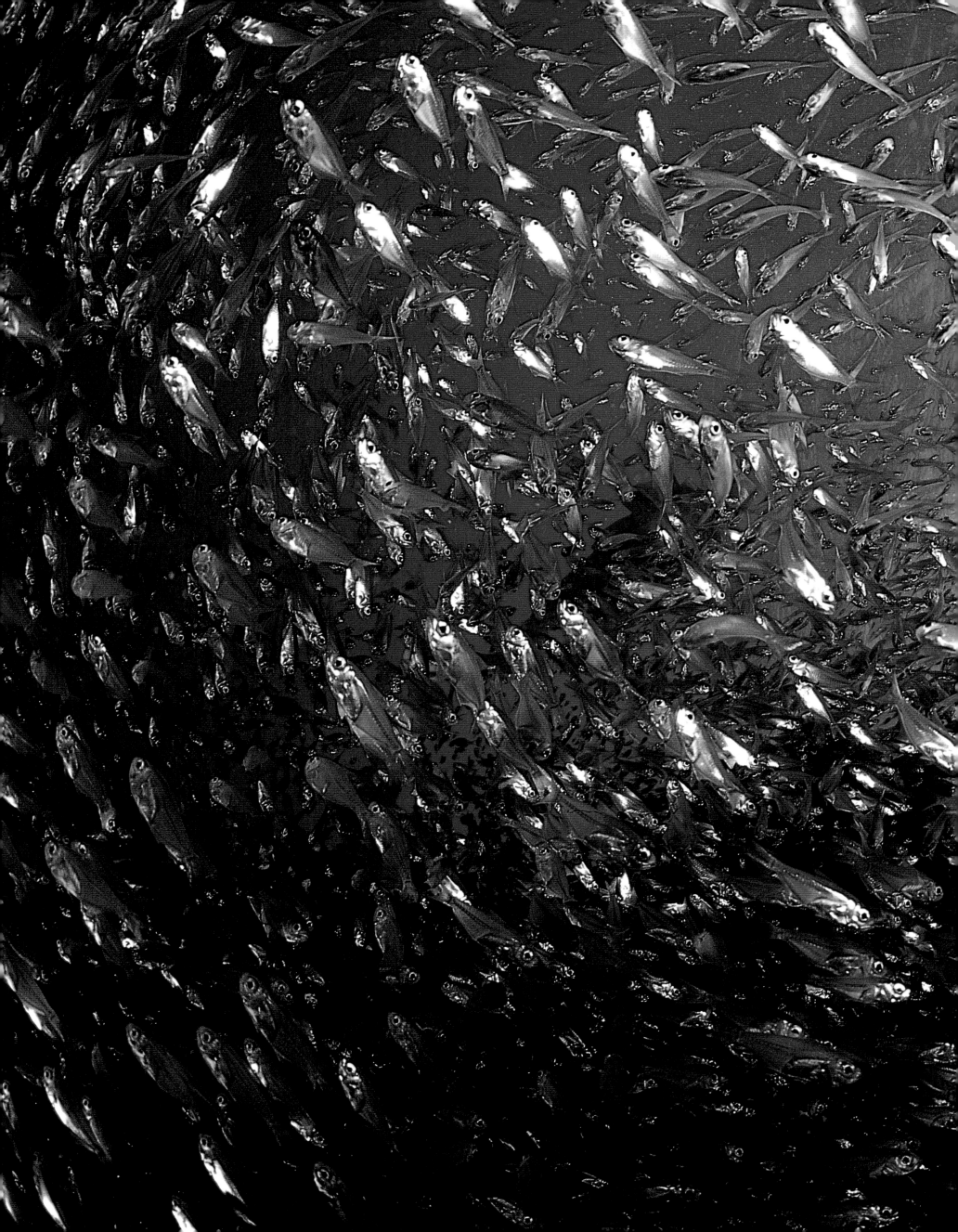

ALDABRA:
THE OCEAN AND
THE INNER LAGOON

It was night-time. The *Fantasea* had left behind the turbulent sea that slowed its progress, and was now making good headway; the moon, which had been shining high in the sky for several hours, illuminated the crest of the waves with sudden gleams, coming and going like will-o'-the-wisps. Just the right atmosphere to make a 30-year-old dream come true.

Thirty years previously I hadn't started diving, although I occasionally explored the sea of my home region of Liguria.

However, I lingered over the pages of *Mondo Sommerso* (Underwater World), the magazine which was the Italian diver's bible at the time; every issue invited the reader to discover unknown worlds, with fascinating stories and splendid pictures of the sea and the terrifying creatures (so it was thought then) that held sway in it.

It was 1964 when I first read about Aldabra, an extraordinary atoll in the Indian Ocean with a huge lagoon, where sharks and crocodiles swam and hunted together (I only found out later that this probably occurred centuries or millennia ago) and thousands of giant turtles lived. The article was prompted by a project generated by the madness of the Cold War. The British to whom the atoll belonged (it was part of BIOT, British Indian

28-29 Although smaller than those found in the Red Sea, the Aldabra gorgonian sea fans, sometimes decorated by a sea lily, sometimes by delicate tufts of Alcyonaria, always make a pretty picture.

Ocean Territory) had decided, by agreement with the Americans, to turn it into a great air and naval base which, together with two more to be built in the Cocos Keeling Islands and on Diego Garcia, was to constitute a kind of *cordon sanitaire* around the USSR.

Various British and American scientific and cultural associations mobilised to fight the project, especially the British Royal Society and the US National Academy. Expeditions to Aldabra were organised to obtain first-hand news about the situation.

The major American and British cultural, scientific and even political publications covered the issue, and the BBC organised a number of debates. A multitude of articles, studies, conferences and congresses endeavoured to show the world that the atoll could not survive such a blow, and one of the most important natural wonders on earth would soon be lost. All this effort would probably have made no impression on the cynical logic of the politicians if an unexpected event had not solved the problem; in 1967 a serious economic crisis hit Great Britain, which shelved the project to build a military base on Aldabra.

Since then, Aldabra has had an eventful history. After the danger was dispelled, the Royal Society did not lose interest in Aldabra, but followed up its studies and research; between 1969 and 1971 it set up a scientific and research station on one of the four islands which enclose the atoll.

When Aldabra was returned to the newly-founded Seychelles Republic by the BIOT in 1976, the government immediately manifested exceptional interest in and awareness of the unique importance of the atoll, and the Seychelles Island Foundation was set up to supervise studies and conservation of the entire archipelago, and especially Aldabra. In 1981 the atoll was declared a special reserve, and in 1982 UNESCO proclaimed it a *World Heritage Site*.

Between 1980 and 1981, the Royal Society's researchers were replaced by experts from the Seychelles Island Foundation. Despite the difficulties involved, the structures have been extended and modernised, and the Settlement research station on Picard Island, not far from the small West Channel pass, is permanently inhabited by a dozen or so rangers. Under the supervision of Patrick Bijou, a very gentle man who loves the place, nature and turtles, the rangers monitor the state of the atoll, record every event and accommodate the researchers who visit it now and again.

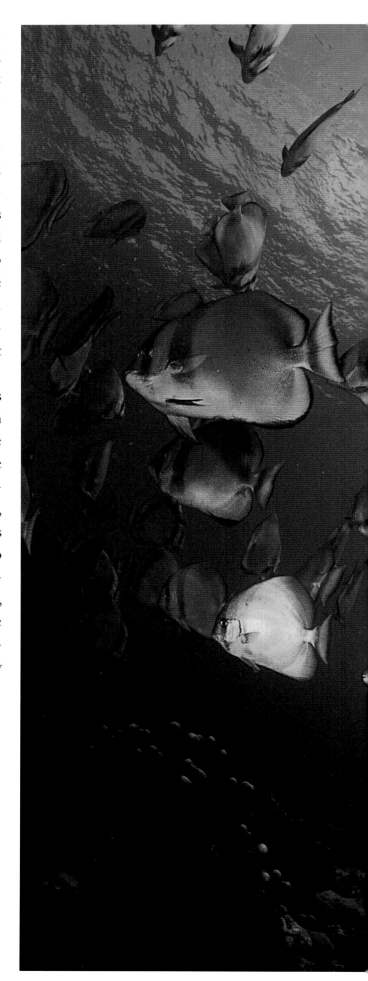

30-31 Batfish *(Platax orbicularis)* are quite common at Aldabra and Astove; they are sometimes seen alone and sometimes in small groups, but most often swim in dense shoals.

31 top left Mullets *(Mulloides vanicolensis)* and snappers *(Lutjanus ehrenbergii)* often mingle to form a single shoal.

31 top right A shoal of trevally *(Caranx sexfasciatus)* is swimming in a dizzying carousel on the plateaux in front of the Settlement.

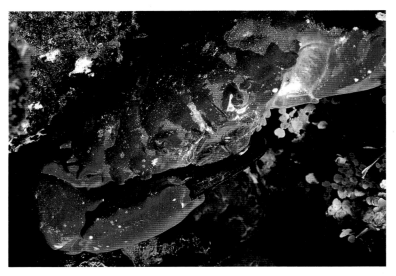

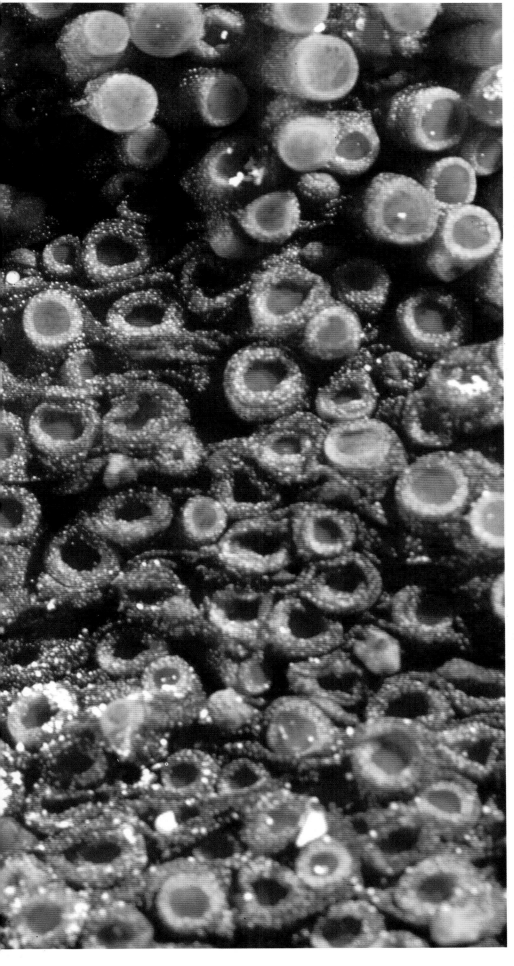

During the same period the dreams generated by the pages of *Mondo Sommerso* began to come true as I visited some of the most spectacular oceans in the world. However, the memory of that long-ago reading must have remained latent in my imagination, so when I heard that Howard Rosenstein (an intelligent, resolute seafarer who had already introduced hundreds of divers to some of the loveliest parts of the Red Sea with his boats) had discovered Aldabra and decided to extend his sphere of operations to the atoll it didn't take me long to make my mind up; I contacted him, and set off on a new adventure.

Since then I've returned to Aldabra several times, always with the same enthusiasm and excitement I can feel bubbling up inside me as after a calm night's sailing we approach land, announced by a flock of boobies flying over the boat. Finally Aldabra appears, low on the horizon, with clouds of a strange greenish colour scudding over it; this is the reflection of the huge lagoon, larger than Mahé, the biggest island in the Seychelles.

It must have looked just the same to the first visitors, the courageous Arab navigators who, at the beginning of this Millennium, gave it the name *Al-khadra* (green) by which it is still known today. Others landed on the islands of the atoll after them, although the first mention on a chart only appeared in 1509, and the first record of a visit dates from 1742; these visitors were mostly sailors who landed to take on supplies of giant turtle meat.

32 top Large red crabs *(Etitus splendidus)* hide among the rocks of Hodoul Point; they are most often encountered during night dives.

32-33 You only need to pick up a holothurian and turn it over to find a few companions like this prawn *(Periclimenes sp.)* nestling in the tortured folds of its skin.

34-35 Two porcelain crabs take refuge in the soft folds of a magnificent sea anemone *(Heteractis magnifica)*.

36-37 At night the usually aggressive clown surgeonfish *(Acanthurus lineatus)* slumbers among the coral, and remains immobile even when a diver approaches.

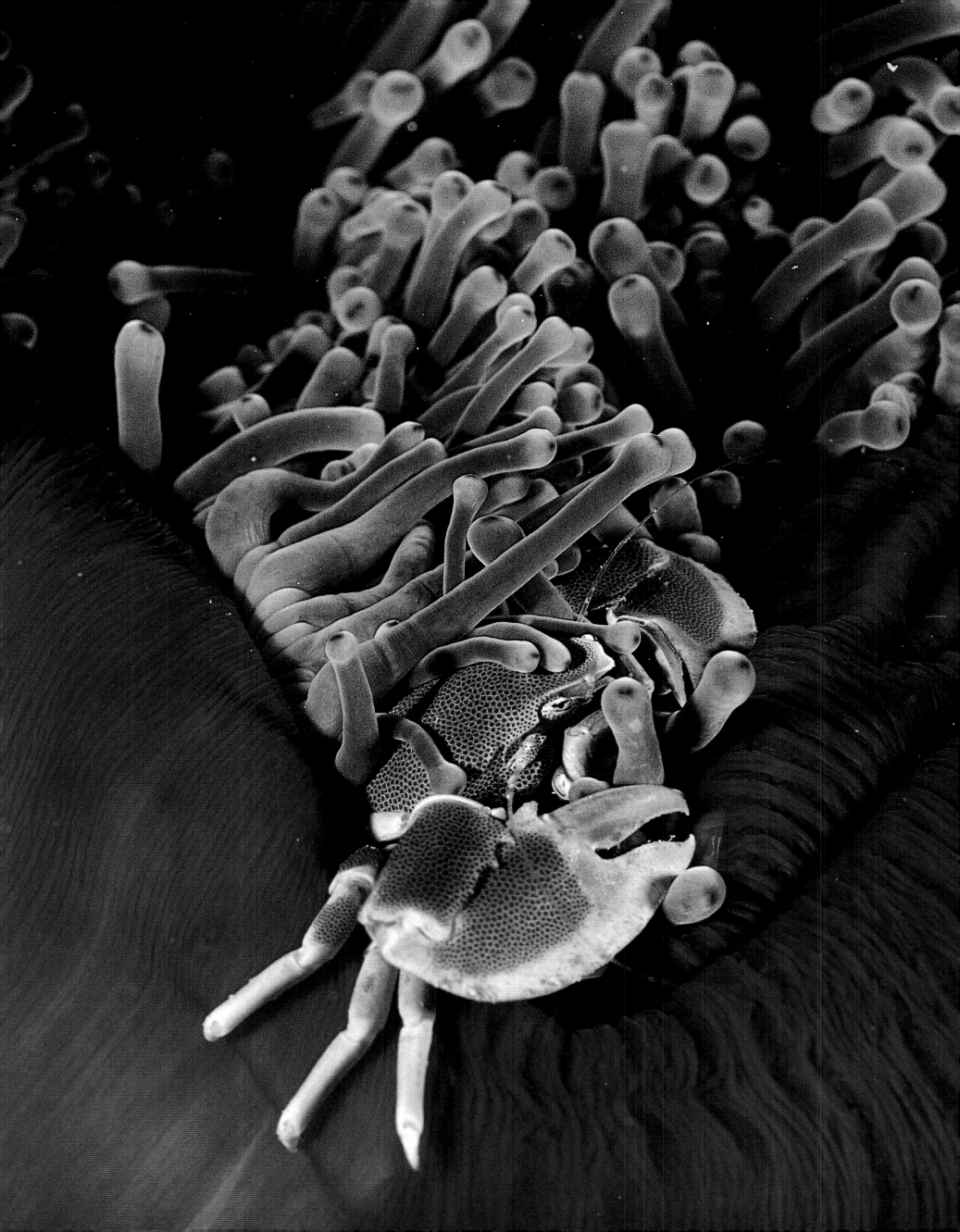

38 top An encounter with a lionfish is less common at Aldabra than in the inner islands. This picture shows a *Pterois volitans* threateningly confronting the camera.

38-39 A *Pterois antennata* exhibits its splendid radiating pectoral fins, joined at the base by a colourful membrane.

Between the 18th and 19th centuries there were some attempts at colonising the islands, but they all rapidly failed because of the scarcity of water, the distance from the usual sea lanes and the difficulty of landing.

Then, at the beginning of the 19th century, researchers realised the scientific importance of the area, and asked the Governor of Mauritius, under whose jurisdiction the atoll then came, to ban or regulate tree felling and turtle hunting. These petitions have been renewed until the present day with some success; according to a recent census over 150,000 giant land turtles now live on the atoll, whereas there are only a few hundred on the more famous Galapagos.

Apart from giant turtles, many other animals live on Aldabra; their numbers are only limited by the laws of nature, favourable or unfavourable weather and social or conflictual relationships with other endemic species. These include the giant or coconut crab *(Birgus latro)* with its strong claws, capable of opening a coconut with no difficulty. This coprophagous creature lives in symbiosis with the giant turtles, devouring their excrement and returning it to the soil already processed and ready to act as an excellent fertiliser. The hermit crab *(Coenobita rugosus)*, which lives in huge colonies in the places where the turtles graze, behaves in the same way. There are also lizards, butterflies and a huge number of insects on the islands; the only mammals, apart from those imported by man, are bats. There are also numerous species of birds – sea and land birds, and even flightless birds. Aldabra is the main nesting site in the Indian Ocean for four species of sea birds: the great frigate bird *(Fregata minor)*, the lesser frigate bird *(Fregata ariel)* which is hard to tell apart from the former, with which it forms a colony of some 10,000 pairs, the red-footed booby *(Sula sula)* and the splendid white sea swallow *(Phaethon rubricauda)* with its beautiful pointed red beak. The frigate birds and boobies nest in the mangroves in the interior of the lagoon, dividing the seasons between them; the frigate bird nests in the dry season, and the booby in the wet season. A characteristic common to all the birds of Aldabra is their great confidence with strangers; perhaps because of the absence of true predators, they are unafraid of man and easily approached.

Aldabra is a huge atoll formed by a ring of four islands: Grand Terre, which covers over two-thirds of the territory from west to north-east, Malabar (middle island) which occupies the northern part, the smaller Polymnie, also to the north, and Picard, on which the Settlement is located, to the north-west.

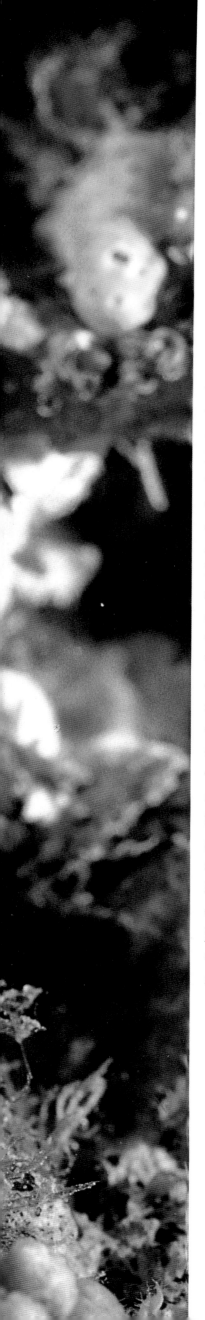

The atoll, which is over 35 kilometres long and 14 kilometres wide, covers an area of 337 square kilometres, over 180 kilometres of which is occupied by a huge lagoon from which some thirty small islands and hundreds of rocks emerge.

Palm trees imported by man at the turn of the century grow along the coast in certain areas, especially on Picard Island; lovely casuarina trees, a member of the pine family with a bright green colour, also grow near Passe Houareau (or East Channel). Thick, low, sometimes almost impenetrable scrub grows everywhere, while mangroves predominate in the lagoon and around the myriad of rocks.

The four passes between the islands, which connect the lagoon to the ocean (West Channel, Main Channel, Johnny Channel and East Channel) allow a huge amount of water to travel in and out with the tide – over half the water which the atoll contains at high tide (some experts believe the figure may be as high as 80%). When the tide recedes, the lagoon empties, leaving huge areas of dry land; rapids flow from one level to another, and the herons feast on trapped fish and small crustaceans. Apart from Main Channel, which is just under 1 kilometre wide at its mouth and over 30 metres deep at some points, the channels are narrow passages, ranging between 16

40 A small blenny (*Ecsenius sp.*) peeps out curiously from its burrow, made from the holes dug by polychaetes in a honeycomb coral.

41 top A prawn is taken by surprise at the entrance to its burrow, and beats a rapid retreat as the diver approaches.

41 bottom Four ring-tailed cardinal fish (*Apogon apogonides*) have nothing to fear from the tentacles of a sea anemone. They usually live in small shoals among the coral, and the males hatch the eggs in their mouths.

metres deep (East Channel) and 8 metres deep (West Channel). Even Main Channel is only navigable by small craft, however; the German battle-cruiser *Königsberg* is said to have lain hidden there during the First World War, before being sunk off the Kenyan coast, but no-one believes the story. Cousteau's *Calypso* tried to enter the channel, but had to make a rapid retreat to avoid being run aground on the coral by the violent current. At high tide, in addition to billions of micro-organisms, even the shallower channels are visited by sharks, sometimes very large ones (I've come face to face, or rather nose to snout, with a bull shark around 3 metres long), barracuda, carangids, turtles and eagle rays which choose the calm waters of the lagoon to hunt, rest or lay their eggs.

When the current is not at the peak of its strength (it can easily exceed 6-8 knots), diving at the mouth of Main Channel and being carried along by the "river" which enters the lagoon is an amazing experience. At first the sea bed is an incredible labyrinth of white dunes, ribs of smooth rock, beds of sand and islands of dead coral, destroyed by the violence of the current; if it were not for the colour, it would look like a moonscape or lava flow. A few large groupers look on curiously as the diver passes by, thick shoals

of carangids, battling against the current, scarcely part, huge sweetlips slither along the sea bed, and a few shy nurse sharks, surprised by the sudden apparition, dart away with a flick of their tails.

After 200 or 300 metres the situation changes; the large plateau splits into four or five channels, and here the most interesting but hectic part of the journey begins. Open-roofed tunnels 10 to 30 metres wide are enclosed between steep, almost vertical walls; the sea bed rises to not more than 6/7 metres from the surface, falls to nearly 30 metres, then rises and falls again several times.

The current and the speed increase and decrease, depending on the width of the passage. You have the feeling of being sometimes dragged along and sometimes halted by a giant hand that amuses itself by continually changing your rate of progress; like travelling on a roundabout plunging up and down the big dipper. It's rather like being at the cinema and watching a film which the director slows down or speeds up, depending on how interesting the scene is; you pass through shoals of fish, glimpse skate and turtles stationary on the sea bed, and look into gaping ravines to see incredible groupers peeping out from the opening and nurse sharks sleeping inside. The visibility is not

42-43 This perhaps unique specimen of a Spanish dancer *(Hexabrancus sanguineus)* grows to over 20 centimetres long. These nudibranchs usually have a red coat with white edging on the "wings", whereas this one has an orange coat, and the inside of the "wings" is bright red. The gill tuft is also orange, but a paler shade.

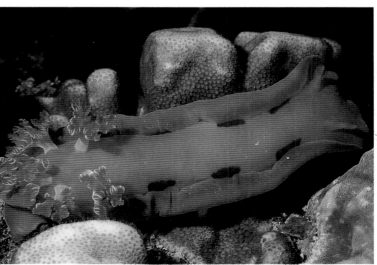

very good because the current drags along algae and organisms in suspension, but the spectacle is incredible, and the feeling indescribable.

After nearly half an hour the channel becomes more uniform, and the depth levels out at around 10 metres. The sea bed looks like a long carpet of pebbles, and the walls, which rise almost to the surface, are teeming with coral-dwelling fish, alone or in shoals, which appear to be extraordinarily active. When you finally re-emerge, you realise that the entrance of the channel is far away (over 3 kilometres) and you've penetrated deep into the lagoon, while the current continues towards the interior, as if it were trying to flow out of the opposite side and return to the open sea.

Diving in the East Channel is nearly as exciting. This single channel is much narrower (no more than 30-40 metres wide) and shallower (not more than 18 metres deep), and ends in a kind of plateau covered with lettuce coral on which a dozen or so huge rhinoceros fish regularly graze, ready to flee at the first sign of danger. En route the sea bed is crossed by changing waves of sand up to 3 metres high, on which you're literally shot forward by sudden accelerations of the current. It's a fantastic feeling, like flying, to be carried along, skimming over the sand, and find yourself face to face with a huge grouper taken by surprise in the hollow of the wave, looking astonished at the sudden apparition.

The coastline of Aldabra is a dramatic sequence of above-water coral formations, eroded by wind, waves and rain; a myriad of rough, eroded mushrooms with chitons resting on them and crabs and small molluscs scuttling over them, interspersed with short, often inaccessible beaches of pale sand.

In order to develop, a coral atoll needs the continual movement of ocean waves, a fairly warm temperature and the play of the currents. Aldabra, which is located in the middle of an ocean, far from the great continental land masses and the larger islands (the closest, Madagascar, is over 600 kilometres away) possesses all these features.

The climate is fairly similar all year round; the wind is never particularly strong, although at some times of year it can exceed 10 knots. Cyclones are very unusual and yearly rainfall seldom reaches 1,200 millimetres. The sea bed all round the island is a gradual slope covered with large coral formations. All the most common species are well represented; splendid acropores of all forms and colours are found nearest the surface, and damselfish

44-45 The colouring and patterns of the parrotfish are highly varied, and the male and female often differ. The specimen shown in the top picture, taken by surprise at night, is a female brown parrotfish *(Scarus niger)* with an amazing arabesque on its snout. The one in the bottom picture is a female *Scarus rubroviolaceus.*

and cardinal fish with varying patterns and shapes dance round them. On the sand, splendid green- or blue-tipped *Stylophorae* are populated by timid damselfish.

A little deeper grows fire coral, and especially Alcyonaria, among which small gobies and transparent prawns hide. Even deeper, over 10-15 metres down, divers will see huge brain coral, the incredible effects of honeycomb coral, the green leaves of lettuce coral, the tortured fins of *Heliopore* and numerous types of leather coral. Numerous umbrellas of Christmas tree worms are to be found on the larger formations; they are smaller and shyer than usual, but incredibly colourful.

A huge number of coral-dwelling fish live among the coral, in some cases leading very hectic lives. A recent study estimates that 185 species of fish are to be found in a 3 square kilometres area of reef. Regardless of the scientists' statistics, divers are bound to be amazed at the number and variety of species: Ray's bream, damselfish, angelfish, butterfly-fish, parrotfish, cardinal fish, fusiliers, wrasse, surgeonfish and triggerfish swim frenetically back and forth without a moment's rest; they come and go, chase one another, eat algae or coral and chase away intruders, and adult and young forms mingle in a kaleidoscope of colours I have rarely seen elsewhere.

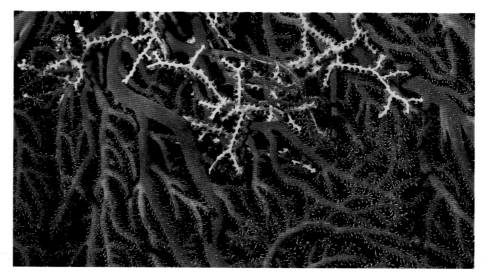

47 top The delicate branches of two gorgonian sea fans are densely entwined, producing an unusual colour contrast.

Whenever a strip of sand appears between the coral formations, splendid mushroom corals appear, with their intriguing colours and mouths, together with fire gobies and beautiful prawn gobies with their magnificent colouring. These fish, which are very difficult to approach, are often associated with a tireless prawn permanently intent on cleaning their common lair. Picasso fish dart around them, always ready to hide if disturbed.

The most striking feature is the extraordinary concentration of fish of the same type; dense shoals of striped snappers, yellow with blue-white stripes, that hardly move when the diver swims up, the shyer humpbacked snappers with their unmistakeable reddish highlights, the restless fusiliers, half yellow and half blue, that amuse themselves by swimming a few times around the guest then disappear as suddenly as they came, and the totally non-migratory goatfish.

Batfish, alone, in pairs, in small groups or in shoals of over 50-100 are also regular companions on every dive. They are very curious, and can even be irritating because they will insist on getting between the photographer and the subject being photographed, as if they were more important.

Above all there are the groupers, a constant, reassuring, characteristic, unavoidable presence. There are red groupers with their sickle-shaped tails, coral groupers, often young but at least half a metre long, shy and suspicious, with wide black stripes and a yellow tail and snout, the marble grouper, the yellow-finned grouper, the white spotted grouper that rests on the sea bed, the fantastic *Dermatolepis striolatus* with its spotted yellow-brown coat, the powerful Malabar grouper, and above all *Epinephelus tukula*, known as the potato cod because its pale coat covered with dark spots resembles potato peel. This magnificent fish, which can easily grow to the same size as the diver, is an almost constant companion during all dives at Aldabra; quiet and trusting, it swims up, stares at you and observes you, seeming to take note of all your movements, disappears slowly under the coral and then pops out again a little way away as if it wanted to make contact or be stroked.

This is not just my imagination. I once saw a very unusual sight at Hodoul Point. A huge potato cod had accompanied me, sometimes in front, sometimes behind, as if it wanted to point out the most interesting things to photograph; it stopped in the water or skimming the bottom when I stopped as if it wanted to see if I was doing things right, if I

48-49 One or two gobies (*Bryaninops youngei*) no more than 3 centimetres long, busy looking for the best place to lay their eggs, are frequently encountered on the branches of the whip corals that grow on the sandy plateaux of Aldabra.

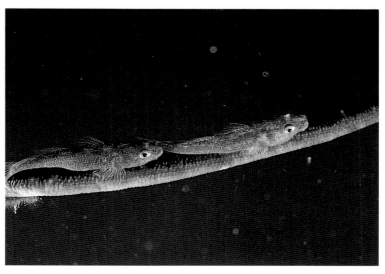

50-51 Numerous species of sweetlips live in the waters of Aldabra. This photo shows a specimen which has the same characteristics as the giant sweetlips *(Plectorhinchus obscurus)*, apart from its unusual yellow lips.

was framing the subject properly and the flashes were correctly positioned. After a few minutes of this game another, slightly smaller grouper emerged from a hole and swam up to us; the two stopped to look at one another for a moment, snout to snout, then accompanied me together, rubbing against one another, side to side, head to head, like two purring cats.

No less common than groupers are the tropical umbras with huge lips known as sweetlips: the huge dark one *(Plectorhinchus obscurus)* which grows to nearly 1 metre long, another slightly smaller one *(Plectorhinchus plagiodesmus)* with yellow lips and a splendid silvery coat with brown stripes, the elegant African sweetlips *(Plectorhinchus pauleyi)*, the *gaterinus* and the *orientalis*, the former yellow with black spots, and the latter yellow with black stripes and leopard-spotted tail and fins.

The first three often travel in convoy, in shoals of 5 to 20; they appear between the coral formations in perennial movement, rising and falling, chasing one another in the water and then swimming down to skim over the sea bed. They are very curious, and .often follow divers throughout a dive. Sometimes, at the entrance to the passes, in front of the Settlement at Hodoul Point, they can

50 bottom left
An African sweetlips
(Plectorhinchus paulayi)
swims along the ocean
floor.

50 bottom right A small
formation of yellow-lipped
sweetlips *(Plectorhinchus
plagiodesmus)* inspects the
coral formations scattered
over the sand, in search
of food.

51 top Giant sweetlips
(Plectorhinchus obscurus)
and yellow-lipped
sweetlips *(Plectorhinchus
plagiodesmus)* swim
together at the entrance
to Main Channel.

51 bottom A group
of giant sweetlips and
black sweetlips
(Plectorhinchus gibbosus)
swim merrily round in
circles at Hodoul Point
reef.

be quite annoying; they come and go non-stop and keep swimming round and round divers, not leaving them alone for a second. You can hardly get rid of them, and if you're not careful all the photographs you take home will show the same subject: sweetlips galore. The *gaterinus* and *orientalis* tend to stay in the same place; they usually swim around the same coral formation and go in and out of the same hole, which they only leave if they are seriously disturbed.

Divers also frequently encounter carangids, such as the huge Aldabra trevally, which swims alone or in pairs, the large-lip trevally which sometimes likes to graze in the sand in search of small invertebrates, the blue-fin trevally that swims in small groups, skimming over the coral, and great shoals of big-eye trevallies and pompanos. In my opinion the pompano, with its strong body covered with a white, almost silvery coat terminating at the yellow fins and large sickle-shaped tail, and its typical pouting snout, is one of the most magnificent creatures of the deep; these fish patrol the entrance to the passes and the sandy plateaux closer to the surface in shoals of several hundred.

As the sea gets deeper, coral formations increasingly give way to strips of sand, which gradually widen until they become predomi-nant. The situation is the same all over Alda-bra, but the approach and depth vary.

To the south the slope ends quite suddenly at around 10-15 metres, 20 at the most, and the sand forms a huge plateau that stretches out to sea as far as the eye can see. This is the home of the shy conger eel, the dream and desperation of underwater photogra-phers; as soon as you get close they disappear underground, and reappear as soon as you move a little way away, always out of camera range.

Above all, this is the kingdom of the sting-ray, which swim alone, in pairs or in groups, sometimes very large ones (I've encountered around 20 on a plateau). These often huge creatures lie hidden under the sand with only their huge eyes peeping out and their sting, over 1 metre long, sticking straight up. If disturbed they sometimes swim off, but more often just move a few metres away, hoping that the intruder will understand their desire to rest and go somewhere else.

To the west, the sea bed slopes gently down to a respectable depth, well over 30 metres. Sea fans begin to appear here; they are not large, often less than one metre tall, much smaller than those generally seen in the Red Sea, but very pretty, decorated with a few branches of colourful Alcyonaria (quite rare

52-53 The Aldabra groupers, especially the potato cod *(Epinephelus tukula)*, are highly sociable; they confidently swim up to divers, and sometimes allow themselves to be touched.

53 top It is not unusual to spot potato cod immobile in their burrows, having their parasites removed by cleaning fish *(Labroides dimidiatus)*.

at Aldabra) and the occasional sea lily, and surrounded by shoals of Ray's bream. Common sights on the sand are the green branches of *Dendrophyllia micranthus* and clumps of two gorgonians with their typical whiplash shape: *Elisella plexauroides* is purple, and *Gorgonella marisrubri* is a more orange colour.

On the north side of the atoll the slope becomes cliff-like and much steeper (25-30 degrees), though it never acquires the structure of a drop-off. At Anse Cèdres, Anse Malabar and Anse Badamier the coral formations, which alternate with strips of sand as if to continue the structure found on the surface, descend rapidly to well over 30 metres deep.

Encounters with migratory fish such as manta rays, eagle rays and sharks are quite common. However, sharks are infrequently seen, and usually not very large; apart from a few hammerheads which are difficult to get close to and a bull shark of respectable size, I have only encountered the occasional small reef shark. Turtles, especially the green turtle (*Chelonia mydas*), are very common, and there is also the occasional hawksbill (*Eretmochelys imbricata*).

The scene changes further east, at Hodoul Point. All round Aldabra the underwater visibility is fairly good, but here, probably because of the currents, it is excellent, or at any rate I've always found it so.

There's a plateau of very pale sand that slopes gently down to the open sea, and over a mile from the coast the depth is no more than 20-25 metres. The plateau is studded with small coral islands rising no more than 6/7 metres from the sea bed, full of lairs, ravines and tunnels where groupers, sweetlips and nurse sharks thrive. Sea anemones are few and far between, and nearly all of the same type (*Heteractis magnifica*). Alcyonaria and crinoids are almost non-existent by day, and I have only found them on sea fans.

I can, however, give the lie to the belief (which I have also seen reported in some scientific publications) that Spanish dancers are not to be found at Aldabra. I have personally encountered three, of three different species, in a single night dive. One was quite ordinary, with the typical pink coat and a splendid prawn hidden among its folds, and another was red with white spots. The third was magnificent, with an amazing orange colour edged with a lovely dark red on the wings, and such a smooth coat that I had trouble with the automatic focus of my camera.

Betty's eyes shine as I talk to her about Aldabra. Betty is an Israeli girl who started diving as a child, and now, nearly 20 years later, is the diving instructor who accompanied us on our first trip to Aldabra. She's a tall, pretty girl with long blonde hair and blue eyes. She has a strong, almost stubborn character which contrasts with great shyness, and is very strict but unusually generous.

At first we tended to clash; she didn't want me going off on my own or spending so much time on a particularly interesting subject that I didn't follow the others but perhaps spent the whole dive concentrating on a single situation. She found it even more amazing that after the dive I might go back on board only to change lens and dive in again straight away, to photograph a prawn I'd found on the coral right underneath the boat. She eventually understood, and generously doubled her diving time, risking her health, so as not to leave me on my own. The descriptions of the dives she gave us before entering the water, accompanied by brilliant drawings on the briefing blackboard, were quite perfect. Betty has dived in many oceans, but the entrance to the Main Channel is one of the best spots in her opinion. And who could disagree with her? You enter a veritable maze of coral with an incredible number of huge sweetlips, some at least three feet long, swimming in it. Shoals of red or yellow grunts swim lazily from one coral formation to another, and several hundred batfish suddenly appear, amusing themselves by swimming under a coral arch. The sight is really weird. Like a swarm of bees, the shoal suddenly elongates and narrows to get through a narrow passage; the fish look like schoolchildren who crowd in front of the gate when the bell rings. Then, when they come out the other side, the shoal resembles a snake, and only regains its natural shape a little later. The game is repeated several times until the fish eventually swim away, taking on a strange position parallel to the sea bed, rather like crazy flying saucers. After a while another shoal appears, even larger if possible, consisting of magnificent pompanos, silvery shapes edged with yellow. They surround the diver in a dizzying carousel, as I've seen barracudas do on other occasions. They swim round and round the diver, forming a kind of wall or cylinder of perfectly aligned shapes which starts from the sea bed and almost reaches the surface.

Then they suddenly swim out to sea and return a little later, more cautiously, as if they were wondering why the intruder's still there and hasn't fled, frightened off by their antics.

60-61 A magnificent filament devilfish *(Inimicus filamentosus)* moves slowly along the sand, "walking" on its pectoral fins, which resemble legs. The spiny dorsal fins are highly poisonous.

60 bottom left Two skate, well camouflaged under the undulating white sand, are resting in front of the entrance to the East Channel, probably in preparation for the hunt.

60 bottom right The leaf scorpionfish *(Taenianotus triacanthus)* has the incredible ability to camouflage itself, changing its colouring to match its habitat.

Towards the centre of the pass the scene changes; large coral formations become more rare, and strips of sand and stones take over, until a large clearing appears, constituting the bottom of a canyon, where large goblet sponges grow and great holothurians rest. You might also see a sleeping nurse shark which takes flight if woken suddenly, destroying the coral with a violent flick of its tail, a huge grouper weighing over 300 kilos, its snout surrounded by a shoal of yellow and black pilot fish, and huge moray eels (- quite rare in other parts of Aldabra) coming out of their lairs.

You only need to stop and look round for a while to realise that this is a kind of junction; far off you may glimpse a shoal of eagle rays circling toward the open sea, and every so often a manta ray passes overhead, making for the entrance to the channel. Of course, it almost goes without saying that the sweetlips continue their tireless whirling around, and potato cod are found everywhere.

Totally different, but no less interesting in my opinion is a swim, this time without breathing apparatus, among the mangroves in the Main Channel, the East Channel or especially the West Channel, particularly in the afternoon, when the sun filters through the vegetation, creating spectacular effects of light and shade. Inside the pass, towards the lagoon, a number of rocks and sand islets just break the surface, and mangroves bury their trunks under the water all round them, creating an incredible labyrinth.

The arched, lead-grey branches protruding from the water, only brightened by the sand deposited on them by the current, form a kind of miniature cathedrals; sunlight filters through their naves, together with the dazzling reflections of leaves on the surface. In the middle, dense shoals of small fish gather and swim around; these are the juvenile forms of snappers (especially *Lutjanus kasmira* and *Lutjanus monostigma*) and gurnard, which spend the first part of their lives here, until they move to the open sea. There are also small groupers, striped sparids with the characteristic dark spot on the side, triggerfish, picasso fish, damselfish and large sweetlips, and every so often a shoal of grey mullet appears, identical to those we're used to seeing in the Mediterranean.

Here too, in just over a metre of water, large fish may be encountered. You will often see a huge skate, the usual nurse sharks, a turtle or a busy small shark pass by. However, the real spectacle is constituted by the plays of light and shade and the reflections, while frigate birds fly shrieking overhead.

64-65 Manta rays *(Manta birostris)* mainly feed on plankton, and prefer waters rich in suspensions, which therefore tend to be cloudy. However, they are quite commonly encountered around the Aldabra passes, where huge amounts of microorganisms are carried by the current.

66-67 Large ocean sharks are not often seen at Aldabra; they are more often encountered on the awesome drop-offs of Astove. These photos show some grey sharks *(Carcharhinus albimarginatus)* of impressive size (they can grow to three metres long), evidently unconcerned by the diver's presence.

68-69 Turtles are commonly found throughout the Aldabra group. Divers will usually encounter the magnificent green turtle *(Chelonia mydas)*, but may also spot a loggerhead *(Caretta caretta)* or a hawksbill *(Eretmochelys imbricata)*. The isolation of the atoll and the variety of the surrounding habitats provides the ideal place for turtles to live, feed and breed.

70 This tiny red shrimp *(Periclimenes sp.)* sometimes lives in association with a cowrie. If you pick up a shell and wait for the disturbed mollusc to go back inside, you may see one of these shrimps come out.

71 A long-nosed flying gurnard *(Oxycirrhites typus)* can often be seen among the delicate branches of red sea fans, cleverly camouflaged as it waits for some unwary victim to pass by.

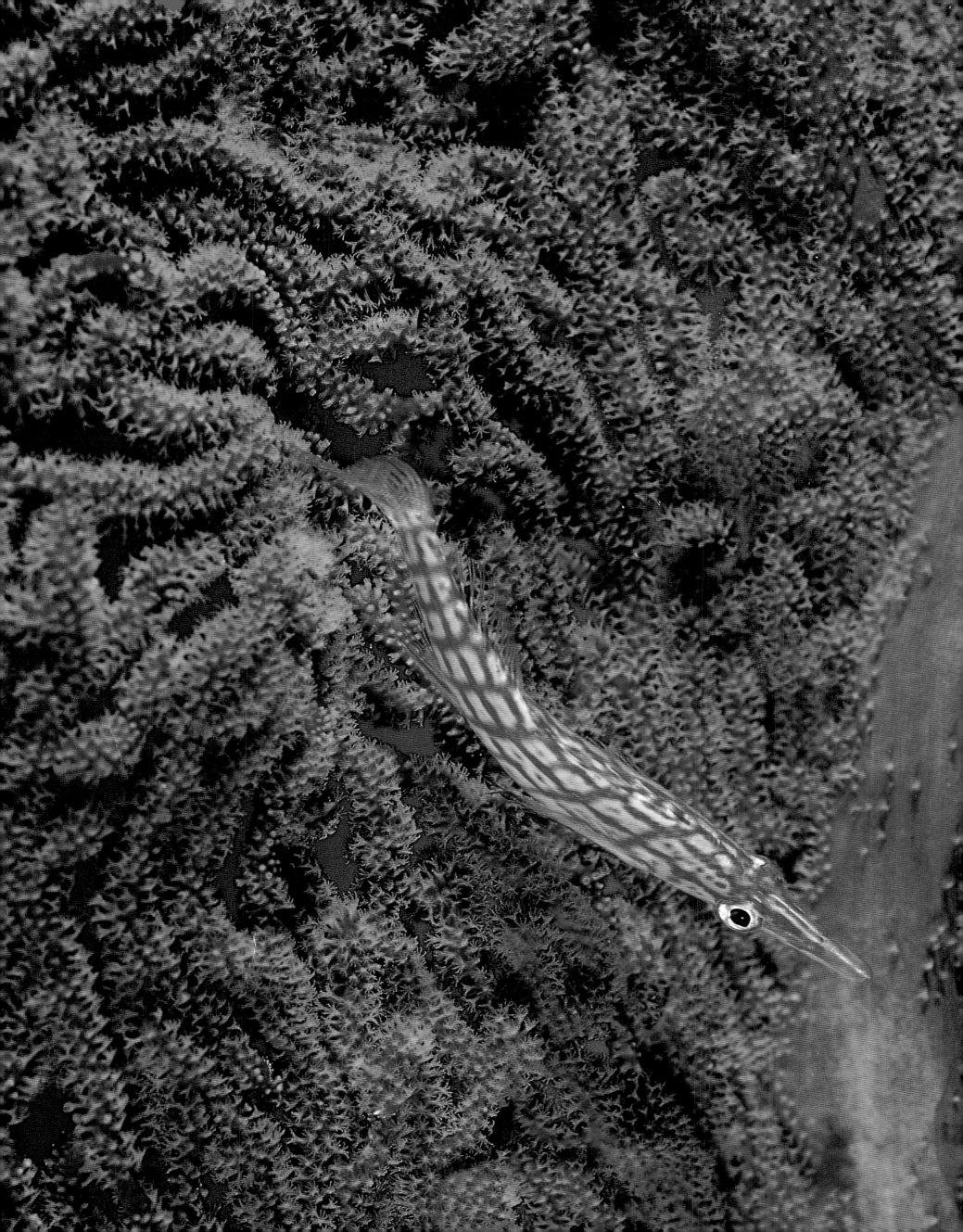

72 Octopus are not very common in tropical waters. However, if you look carefully among the crevices in the coral, you may see one cleverly camouflaged to match the colours of the environment in which it is concealed.

73 This photo shows a poisonous sea snake *(Myrichthys maculosus)* scouring the reef in search of prey. This snake is greatly feared by the smaller fish, which often flee in terror at its approach.

74-75 Clams are some of the largest bivalve molluscs to be found in the sea. As can be seen in this macrophoto, the mollusc has a brightly coloured fleshy mantle. These shells are often found among the coral, in shallow water and in full light.

76 A scorpionfish
(*Scorpaenopsis
oxycephala*), immobile
on a rock and perfectly
camouflaged, waits for
a victim to come within
striking distance of its
mouth.

77 This leaf scorpionfish
(Taenianotus triacanthus)
is almost invisible among
the seaweed, whose
colour it has adopted.

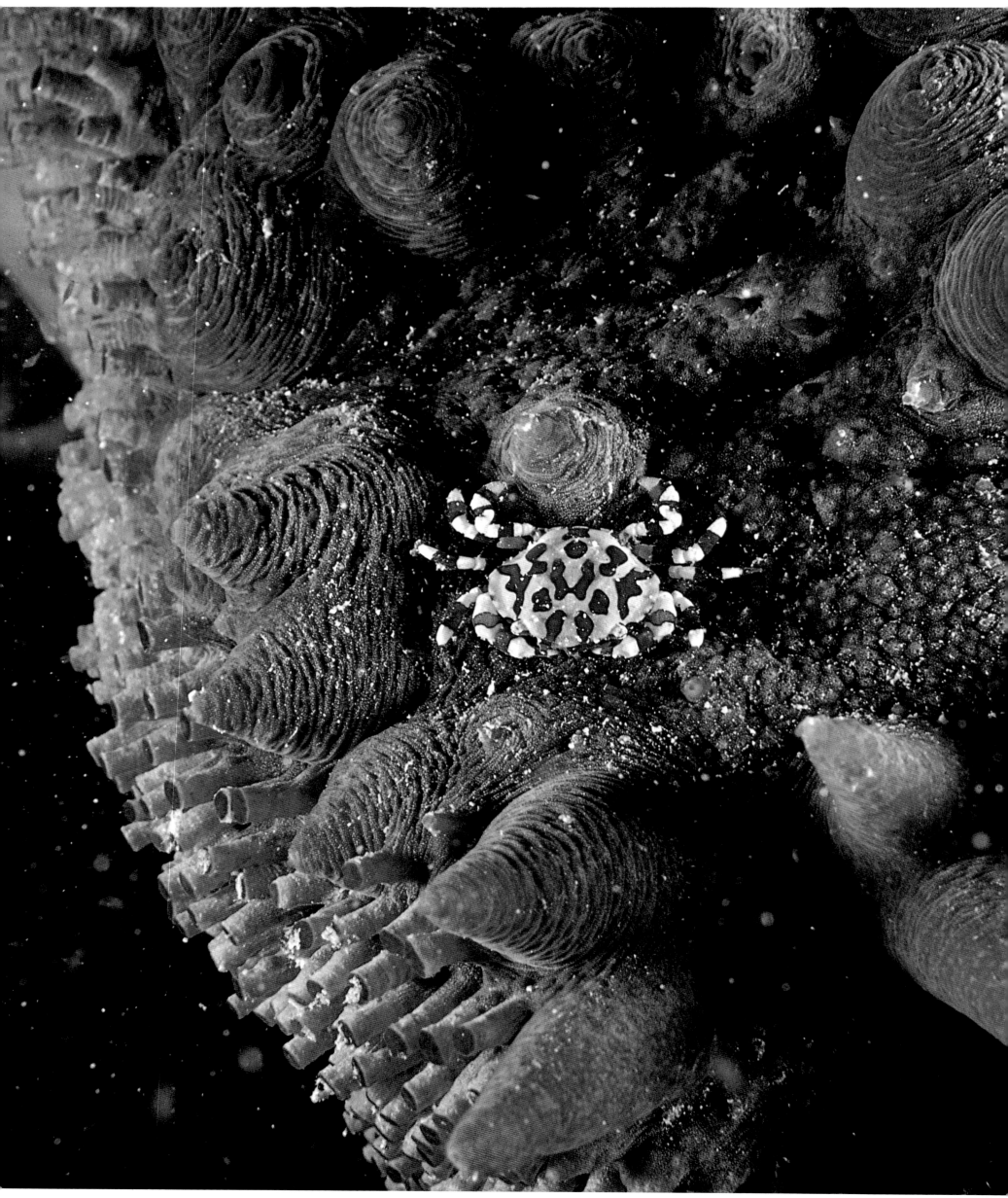

78-79 Holothurians, also known as sea cucumbers, come in numerous shapes and colours. Many live in symbiosis with shrimps or, as in this case, with tiny colourful crabs, which probably eliminate parasites from the skin of these echinoderms.

79 top Sea lilies are believed to be the surviving ancestors of the sea urchins; there are over 650 known species, almost indistinguishable from one another. Tiny fish *(Discotrema echinophila)*, just over a centimetre long, which adopt the colour of their host, sometimes live among the branches.

79 bottom This hard coral of the *Fungia sp.*, with its alarming "mouth", is the only known coral which is non-colonial and not attached to the sea floor.

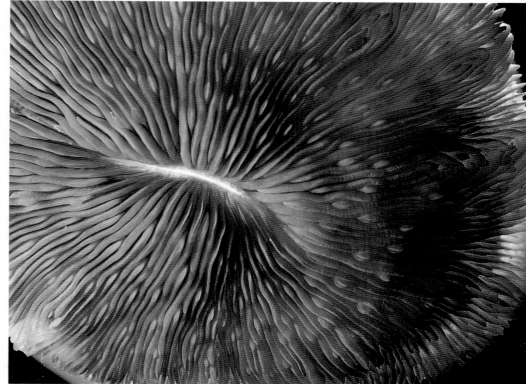

80-81 These photos show the body of the sea anemone *(Heteractis magnifica)*, with its bright colours and soft shapes, in great detail.

82-83 A small goby *(Bryaninops sp.)* hides on the trunk of an Alcyonaria *(Dendronephthya sp.)*, taking advantage of the camouflage effect provided by the multitude of "commas" on the translucent body of this anthozoan.

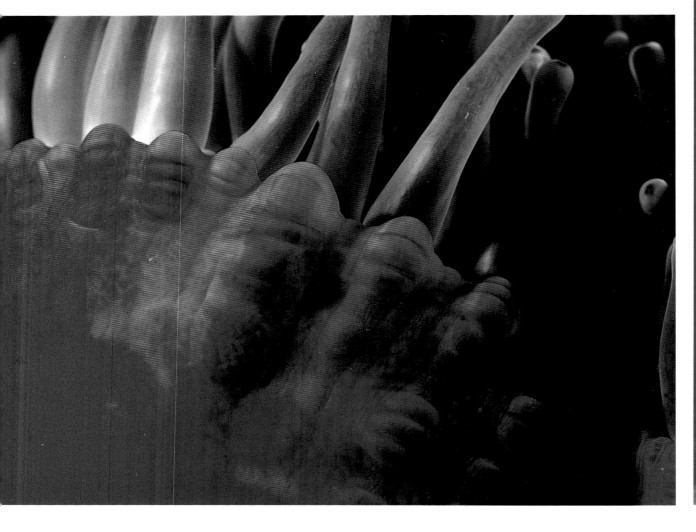

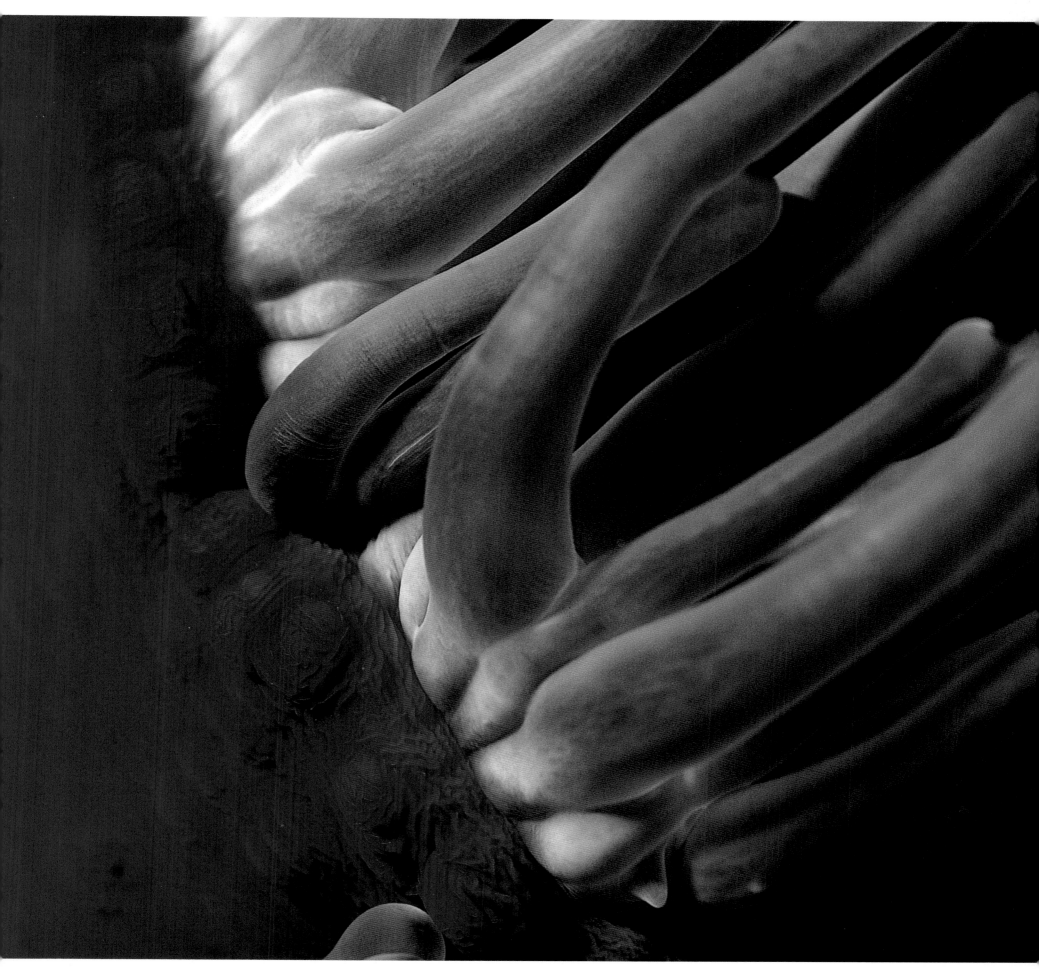

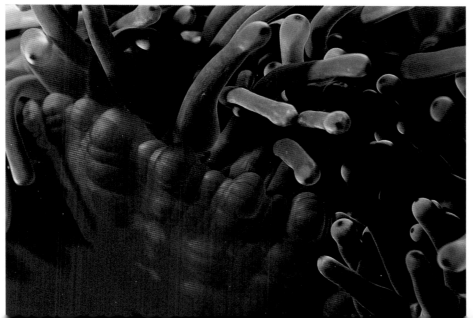

84-85 This unusual photo shows a flying gurnard *(Paracirrhites forsteri)* leaning on a coral branch as if looking out of a window, as it receives a visit from a small damselfish.

85 This moray eel *(Gymnothorax sp.)*, which glares out from the opening of its lair, its terrible jaws open wide, seems to threaten the photographer.

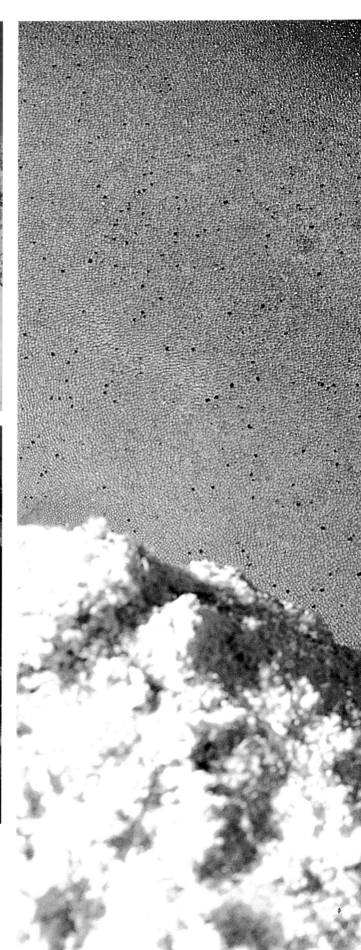

86-87 The nurse shark (*Nebrius ferrigineus*) is a very common sight on the plateaux in front of the passes, at Hodoul Point, and inside the Aldabra lagoon. These sharks sometimes sleep so soundly in caves that divers can touch them. Sometimes, however, these rather shy creatures lie in the sand only apparently asleep, ready to swim off with a vigorous flick of their tails at the diver's approach.

88-89 Dense shoals of snappers (usually *Lutjanus monostigma*, mingling with *Lutjanus ehrenbergi* and *Lutjanus fulvus*) are encountered in the inner lagoon of the Aldabra atoll. Other common sights are red mullet, parrotfish, shoals of grey mullet hunting for food, and big skate dozing in the sand. The fish shown in the photo at the top left probably lost its tail to a predator.

90-91 In the inner lagoon of Aldabra, the tide rises to such a height that it completely covers the leaves of the mangroves.

ASSUMPTION, ASTOVE AND COSMOLEDO: THE DEVELOPMENT OF THE ATOLLS

Assumption, Astove and Cosmoledo are part of the Aldabra group; they are also of coral formation, but have a different structure. Assumption is a roughly aubergine-shaped island, while the other two are atolls which have reached different stages of formation. Astove is at an earlier stage of development; the inner lagoon is surrounded on all sides by a large mass of dry land, with a single small channel leading to the ocean. Cosmoledo is at more advanced stage; there is very little dry land, only a chain of quite separate small islands, and the lagoon covers over 80% of its territory. Both have a very shallow lagoon, only a very small part of which is suitable for sailing. Large colonies of boobies live on the Cosmoledo islands, whereas birds are almost non-existent on Astove and Assumption; needless to say, this is the fault of man. In view of their large land masses, boobies chose Astove and Assumption as their favourite habitat, creating huge reserves of guano. Man has exploited this resource since the mid-19th century; over half a million tons were taken from Assumption alone in a fifty-year period. While they were there, the men cut down trees for firewood, hunted birds and killed turtles for food. The result is that there is no more guano there, but there are no more birds either.

92-93 The soft corals of Cosmoledo are not large, but as a result of the incessant current on the plateaux and the edges of the drop-offs they are swollen and colourful, and play host to numerous life forms.

As a result of action by the Seychelles government, the few inhabitants still living on Assumption no longer hunt turtles, which have recommenced their journey up the beaches (especially the beautiful wide crescent-shaped beach on the east side of the island) to lay their eggs. A reafforestation project is also under way, and a good concrete runway for light aircraft has been constructed, which makes it easier to visit Aldabra.

It's no longer necessary to sail the length of the Seychelles as it was on my first visit, because you can get the boat here, only three hours away from Aldabra, saving a three- or four-day crossing.

Visitors can stay on Assumption; there isn't an actual hotel, but accommodation is provided by a kind, smiling lady in her modest but delightful home.

Astove is uninhabited, and turtles also come up the beaches to lay their eggs there.

However, some visitors to the island still hunt them, and a few hundred are believed to be killed every year, as witnessed by the numerous shells abandoned on the edges of the lagoon – pathetic stinking husks that once protected a living creature.

94 top In the waters of Assumption, only a few metres down, a dense shoal of mullet *(Mulloides vanicolensis)* glides elegantly just above a group of snappers *(Lutjanus monostigma).*

94 bottom Snappers *(Lutjanus monostigma)* and oriental grunts *(Plectorhinchus orientalis)* jointly patrol madrepore formations which have grown almost to the surface.

94-95 These snappers
(*Lutjanus kasmira*),
which are easily
recognisable by the four
blue stripes on their
yellow coat, usually live
and swim in dense shoals.

95 top This photo shows
another dense shoal of
fish; these are fusiliers
(*Caesio sp. caerulaurea*).

96-97 This dense shoal
of silver barracuda
(*Sphyraena qenie*) usually
swims in the waters of
Astove, on the edge of
the drop-off.

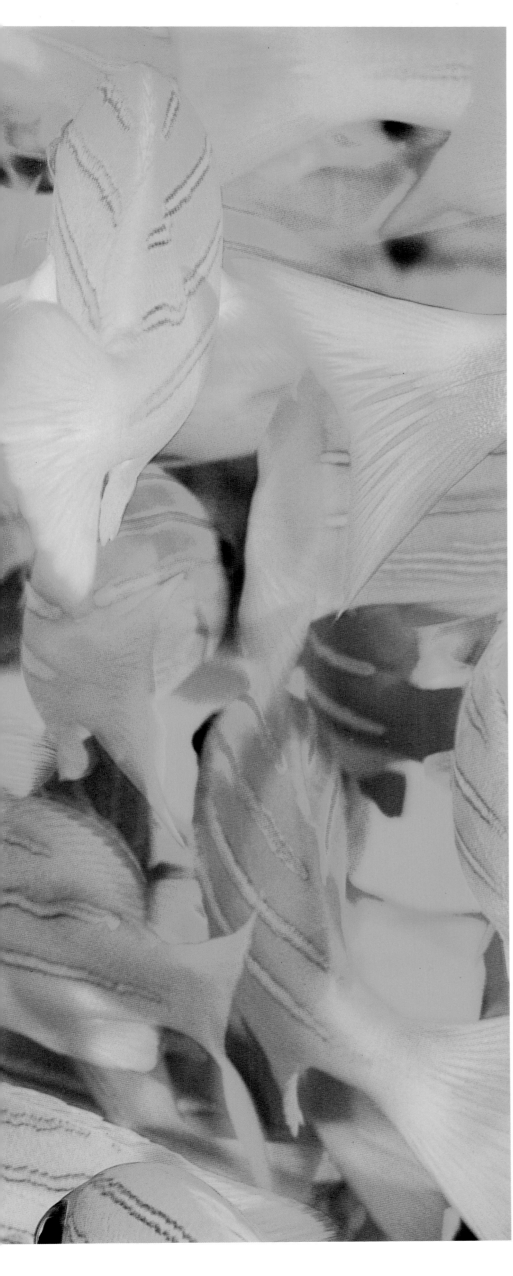

Unlike Aldabra, which rests on a plateau and is therefore surrounded by fairly shallow water, Cosmoledo and particularly Astove are veritable pinnacles rising from great depths.

As a result, the underwater scene is quite different from Aldabra; especially at Astove there are very steep drop-offs, vertical walls that disappear into the ocean, penetrated by crevices, grottoes and caves up to several metres deep. Common sights inside them include sleeping turtles, groupers conscientiously submitting to cleaning by a wrasse that specialises in this task, and shoals of squirrelfish and soldierfish. The steepest area begins in the northern part, especially on the eastern side. There's an anchor chain that's been there goodness knows how many years, which starts from the shore and runs down the wall to a depth of about 50 metres, covered with sponges and magnificent clumps of Alcyonaria populated by anthias, and above all some magnificent flying gurnards. Just below it is a branch of black coral over three metres tall. Further along the wall shoals of carangids and barracuda pass by, and manta rays and sharks can be glimpsed.

There is no lack of unforgettable encounters. One day I was returning to the surface after quite a fruitful excursion on the wall, and I still had three or four photos left to take.

98-99 This dense blue and yellow cloud of striped snappers (*Lutjanus kasmira*) makes a very colourful sight on the Assumption plateau.

I was about to use them up on a turtle sleeping in a grotto less than 10 metres deep when a kind of premonition convinced me to wait a bit longer, and not waste them on what is now a common sight. This was lucky because, when I reached a depth of less than 6 metres, I saw a long rod emerging from behind a coral; I swam up and saw a small plateau with four great rays on it, snout to snout like a huge four-leafed clover, half buried in the sand.

I used up the remaining three photos in a trice. As I swam up to the surface I remembered an annoying incident that had happened at Aldabra a few days earlier; I'd encountered a dozen rays sleeping on a sandy plain, but a careless fellow diver had frightened them away before I got within camera distance.

However, the best dive, and one of the most interesting in the whole area, is further south, where the Astove coral reef suddenly stretches out towards the open sea. There's a saddle-back reef with some splendid formations interspersed with strips of white sand.

The stars of the reef are the pompanos, those magnificent creatures that play with the diver, brush against him, envelop him in a huge, spectacular, silvery veil, hover in the water to scrutinise him and weigh him up with their eyes, then swim down to rub themselves luxuriously against the sand.

100 Alcyonaria or soft corals are one of the most common underwater sights in the Indian Ocean. Some particularly fine specimens can be seen in the waters of Cosmoledo.

101 This scorpionfish (*Scorpaenopsis venosa*), with its rather unusual colouring, is resting comfortably on a leather coral, waiting for a victim to pass by.

102 The delicate, swollen tentacles of a sea anemone protect a pair of Seychelles clownfish (*Amphiprion fuscocaudatus*).

103 Unlike other clownfish, which are highly aggressive and do not hesitate to attack divers, this Seychelles clownfish (*Amphiprion fuscocaudatus*) is very shy, and hides among the tentacles of an anemone in company with a tiny transparent shrimp.

104-105 In the waters of Assumption, the activities of some tiny creatures, such as this attractive spotted anemone crab (*Neopetrolisthes maculatus*) or a tiny shrimp (photo at bottom right), can be observed among the short tentacles of a carpet sea anemone (*Stichodactyla mertensii*).

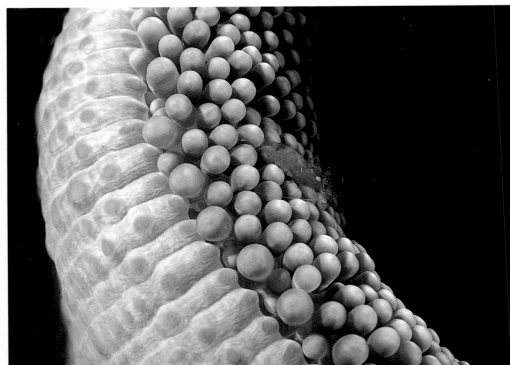

106 In the waters of Astove, a diver hovers above a huge coral formation on which a delicate branch of soft coral has grown.

106-107 The Alphonse drop-off is covered with a "hedge" of sea fans. The one shown in this photo has been oddly colonised by a myriad of brittle stars.

108-109 Sea anemones often grow and develop in colonies. The ones shown in this photo *(Heteractis magnifica)* are inhabited by a group of domino damselfish *(Dascyllus trimaculatus)*, still in the juvenile phase.

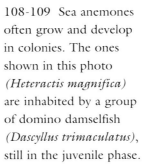

Pompanos are not alone, but accompanied by a school of magnificent barracuda circling high on the edge of the drop-off, a shoal of majestic batfish and a shoal of large-eyed jacks. The barracuda are shyer, keeping their distance from the pompanos; the jacks are more sociable, and the batfish in particular don't mind mingling with the others, then swim off and regain their independence at an imperceptible signal from the leader of the shoal.

We are not very deep here, and the current is usually not very strong unless you approach the drop-off; you can therefore enjoy the dive to the full, with no worries, and stay down for a considerable time. It's not until you emerge that you realise that you haven't been able to devote sufficient attention to the splendid coral formations, the huge sea anemones populated by clownfish, sometimes visited by beautiful porcelain crabs, and the colourful permanent population.

If you continue south, following the ridge that slowly approaches land, you have to cope with a stronger current, but to make up for it there are numerous colonies of thick red tortured sea fans populated by shoals of damselfish with their permanently undulating movement, resembling that of the waves.

110 There are numerous burrows inhabited by moray eels in the waters of Assumption. The top photo shows a leopard moray *(Gymnothorax undulatus)*, and the bottom photo shows a white-mouth moray *(Gymnothorax meleagris)*.

110-111
The white-mouth moray *(Gymnothorax meleagris)*, which is common in some areas of the Indo-Pacific, is quite rare in the Seychelles. The white spots on its coat sometimes form a lattice pattern.

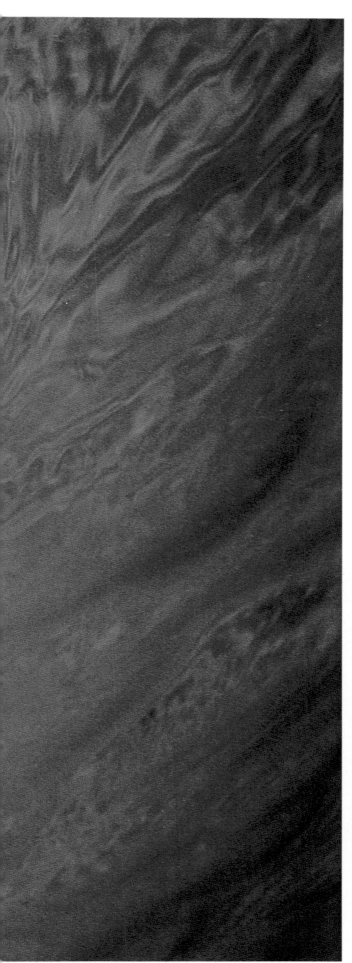

112-113 A green turtle *(Chelonia mydas)* that has just left the nest tries desperately to reach the open sea, where it can hide from attacks by predators and grow to adulthood.

113 A magnificent loggerhead turtle *(Caretta caretta)*, caught by surprise as it searches for its usual food – small crustaceans and molluscs.

Diving at Cosmoledo is not on the same level, but still interesting. I didn't encounter the shoals usually found at Astove, but once again there were lots of Alcyonaria, red sea fans, migratory fish, groupers, and triggerfish hatching their eggs by blowing on them.

An unusual feature are colonies of albino sea anemones with equally white clownfish. Here, the current is quite strong, and diving is often less peaceful; as you swoop along the edge of the drop-off, looking towards the open sea, a shoal of carangids may part to reveal a majestic, regal hammerhead shark, as has happened to me, or a patrol of grey reef sharks.

Assumption is different again. The boat drops anchor at the half-derelict quay built in the crescent of the east coast, where guano ships once tied up. You dive under the boat, and nearly always end up asking the captain not to move her as long as you stay at the island. The plateau is 6-10 metres down, but immediately plunges to 30 metres and more. However, you can fill all the available time with new encounters without going down so deep. There's a multitude of small life forms;

the coral is teeming with gobies and prawns, small moray eels of various kinds emerge from their lairs, huge sole sleep in the sand, an anemone perches on every coral, and snipefish swim here and there.

You can tell the drop-off's immediately underneath, because migratory fish arrive very often; large groupers rub themselves against the sand, and one or more manta rays turn up nearly every day, in the morning or evening. One of these which I met one day aroused my curiosity; there was something familiar about it that I couldn't place. It wasn't until I developed my photos that I realised it was the same one I'd seen and photographed two days earlier at Aldabra; it had the same crescent-shaped scar on one of its wings, caused by a predator's bite.

Although night dives at Astove and Cosmoledo are entirely satisfactory, they're absolutely magnificent at Assumption.

There's no risk that you won't use up your entire film; in fact it'll run out all too quickly, there are so many different subjects to take. Everything that seems to be lacking in Aldabra at night exists here in plenty.

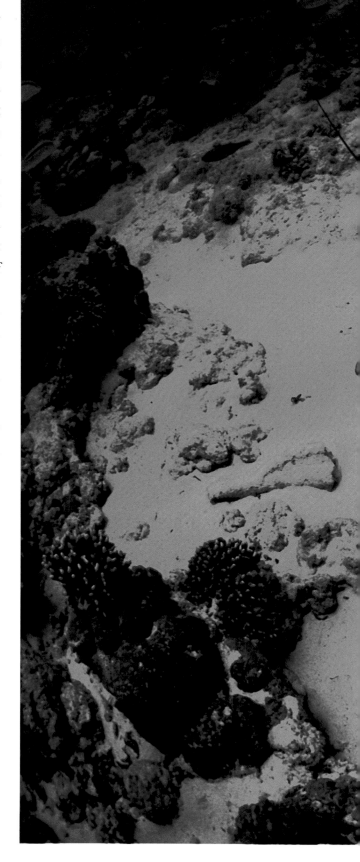

114-115 Four magnificent skate (*Himantura fai*) resting in a few metres of water at the top of the Astove drop-off. One of the fish, perhaps disturbed by the photographer, tries to camouflage itself better in the narrow sandy plateau.

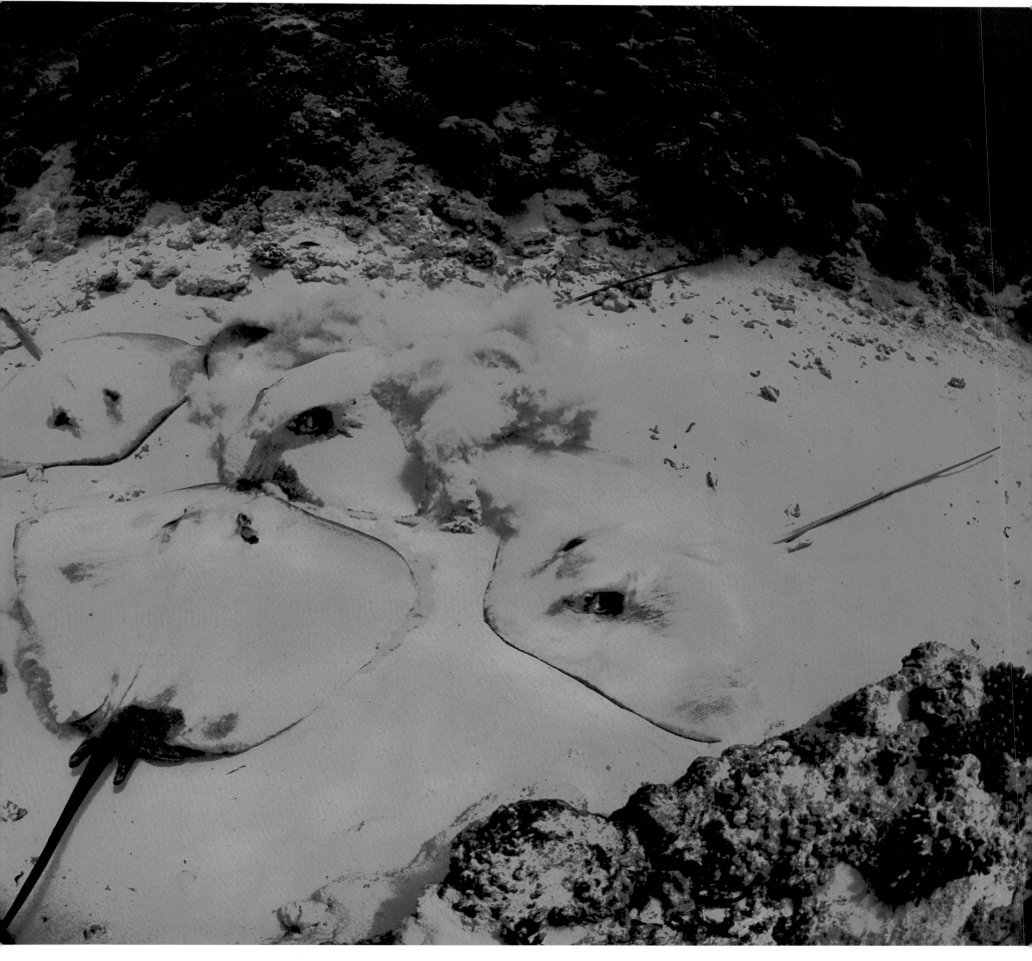

116-117 This huge
tropical turbot *(Bothus
mancus)*, easily
recognisable by its large,
slightly raised spots, can
be found on the sea bed
at Assumption,
motionless and well
camouflaged in the sand.

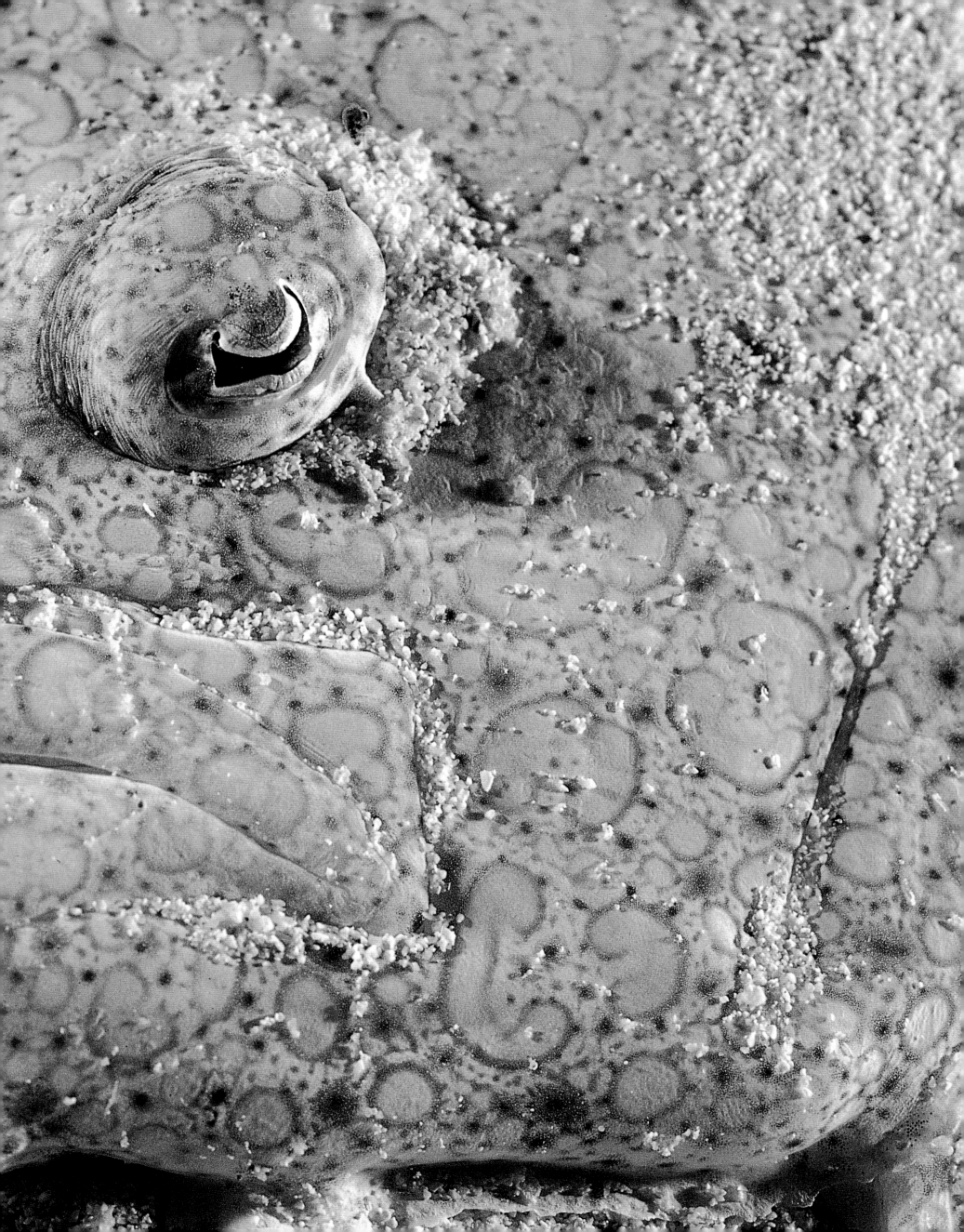

118-119 A blackspotted
torpedo ray (Torpedo
fuscomaculata) disturbed
by the photographer
swims off, leaving a trail
of the sand under which
it was hidden.

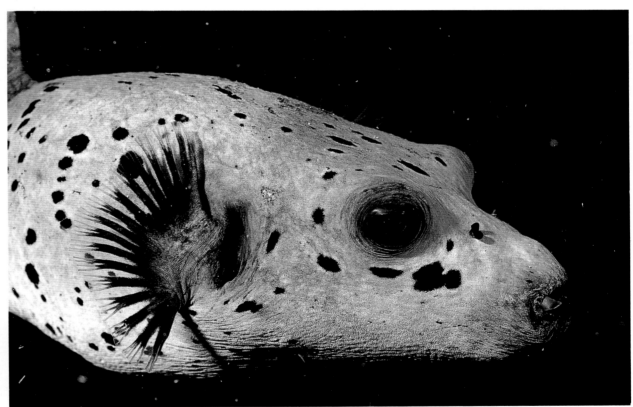

119 Puffers, so called
because they puff up
when disturbed, often
live in the shelter of the
reef, where they hide if
threatened. Two different
specimens can be seen in
these photos; the top
photo shows a starry
puffer *(Arothron
meleagris)*, and the
bottom photo shows a
blackspotted puffer
(Arothron nigropunctatus).

120-121 Some magnificent red gorgonian sea fans, under a metre tall, can be seen during dives at the Cosmoledo reefs; they sometimes grow on the sand, and are sometimes associated with different types of coral. These sea fans flourish because of the plankton-rich current which is usual on these reefs.

122-123 The macrophotography technique shows every tiny detail of the mantle of a huge holothurian.

THE INNER ISLANDS: CORAL GARDENS ON A GRANITE FLOOR

Until the early Seventies, the Seychelles could only be reached by sea. When the airport was opened at the end of 1971, the islands became a milestone in my diving history. Until then I'd dived without breathing apparatus, generally to look at the fish, and occasionally, I regret to say, harpoon them. Breathing apparatus and camera were still in the future. The only sea I knew personally was the Mediterranean; tropical seas were no more than a wonderful dream, cultivated only in my imagination, nurtured on books and magazines. A friend of mine was the grandson of a general who, as a reward for his wartime services, had been appointed custodian of the ossarium on Asinara, a magnificent island just north of Sardinia, then closed to ordinary mortals because of the penitentiary located on it. My friend managed to get permission to visit the island and we spent a week in that unspoilt environment, swimming among shoals of grey mullet and amberjacks, discovering holes full of giltheads and white bream, encountering giant sea bass and sunbathing on magnificent white sandy beaches surrounded by pink granite rocks. One autumn evening a few months later, over an excellent meal of grilled fish, I blurted out the news I'd learned a few hours earlier. An airport had been opened, and it

was possible to reach the Seychelles, islands with white beaches and pink granite rocks, just like Asinara. Should we go? I didn't notice how vague his reply was, and spent the next few days rushing around and visiting travel agents. Eventually I found out what I wanted; yes, the trip could be organised.

My friend turned out to be afraid of flying and backed out, but I wasn't put off, and a few months later, on a bright August morning, I landed at Victoria airport.

124 A pair of soldierfish (*Myripristis vittata*), recognisable by the white line on the fins and the unusual dark spot on the eye, live in a grotto at Shark Rock, in the inner islands.

125 A pair of clownfish (*Amphiprion akallopisos*) shyly peep out from between the tentacles of an anemone (*Heteractis magnifica*).

That very afternoon I donned my mask and flippers and slid into the water off the Danzilles Rocks. A striped surgeonfish darted right in front of my face (this is my first memory of diving in the Seychelles, and I have never forgotten it) followed by a small group of Moorish idols and immediately afterwards a dozen of so huge rhinoceros fish, forming a kind of wall, which swam off, not very concerned by my intrusion. I realised then that the die was cast; I'd never hunt another fish again. I'd hang up my spear gun forever, and the first two things I'd do when I got back to Genoa would be to enrol for a scuba diving course and buy a *Nikonos* camera. All of which I duly did.

The next week passed as if in a dream: the splendid beaches of Mahé, sometimes beaten by the waves, sometimes calm and peaceful, depending on the wind, where you can sunbathe and chat with the calm, relaxed Seychellois; the lush vegetation, an incredible natural botanical garden where all the plants grow to a huge size; trips into the interior, climbing up the roads that cross the island in many places, passing by old colonial houses, through veritable tunnels of greenery, finding myself suddenly face to face with enormous smooth granite rocks, and meeting lovely, polite, helpful people with shy, curious, bright-eyed children. Then I visited Praslin, with the Vallée de Mai where the huge rustling *coco de mer* palm grows, black parrots whistle and hummingbirds flutter, and Cousin Island, the realm of the long-tailed tropic bird which builds its nest on the ground and looks as if it were wearing eye make-up, and the fairy tern, chosen by *Air Seychelles* as its symbol, a small sea bird with immaculate plumage and a sharp blue beak which lays a single egg, leaving it balancing precariously on a branch. When it hatches, a soft fluffy chick waiting for food remains suspended over the void until it learns to fly. Lastly, I made a trip to Curieuse, another small island near Praslin, with some of the loveliest and most characteristic granite formations in the archipelago, where the reproduction of the giant turtle is now protected.

I've gone back to the Seychelles twice since then, but only on a flying visit; I was prevented from diving by lack of time and the unfavourable season. I was not able to dive there again until this year, and it was a very pleasant surprise.

The Seychelles are well known in Europe as a dream resort, a paradise of nature, environment, sun and sea. However, the underwater environment is very little known; divers tend to choose other resorts, which are certainly beautiful but perhaps just more often advertised and better presented. This is a pity in my opinion, because the Seychelles offer one of the most interesting diving experiences, which is special and unusual in many respects.

I can confidently say that the more expert a diver is, the more places he has visited and the more experience he has gained in various parts of the world, the more he will appreciate the beauty and uniqueness of the underwater environment and life of the Seychelles. There are some drawbacks, of course; sometimes the wind causes a rough sea, the water is cloudy and photographers are penalised, and at some times of the year the water is full of plankton which reduces visibility, but attracts numerous whale sharks. However, if you choose the right months, when the sea is calmer and the water clear (March, April and May, September, October and November, but there are variations from zone to zone, so it's best to find out in advance), the Seychelles are the equal of anywhere in world.

All the islands stand on a plateau, which rarely descends to more than 50 metres deep. In fact the islands and the numerous rocks sticking out of the sea rise from depths of no more than 20-30 metres. As a result diving is not difficult; the only problem in some cases may be the currents, although they are not particularly strong.

The underwater environment is special, indeed unique; it appears more Mediterranean than tropical, or rather a curious mixture of both. The most unusual feature of the view which strikes tourists visiting the Seychelles are the huge granite rocks scattered over the beaches: smooth and soft, some lying on the sand, some pointing towards the sky, they look like ancient sculptures made by a giant hand, probably a predecessor of Hans Arp or Henry Moore. Some are grey, some tend towards pink or yellow, and some are darker with black streaks, but all of them are smooth, washed by the millennia, and occasionally decorated by a climbing plant.

This environment and this scene are repeated underwater. There are the same smooth rocks, which the sea has painted in different colours (red, yellow, green, pink and orange) and decorated with threads of whip coral, small white sea fans and colonies of *Tubastrea* corals.

130-131 Sister Bank, between Félicité Island and the Sisters, is a veritable carpet of *Heteractis magnifica* sea anemones, inhabited by clownfish (*Amphiprion akallopisos*).

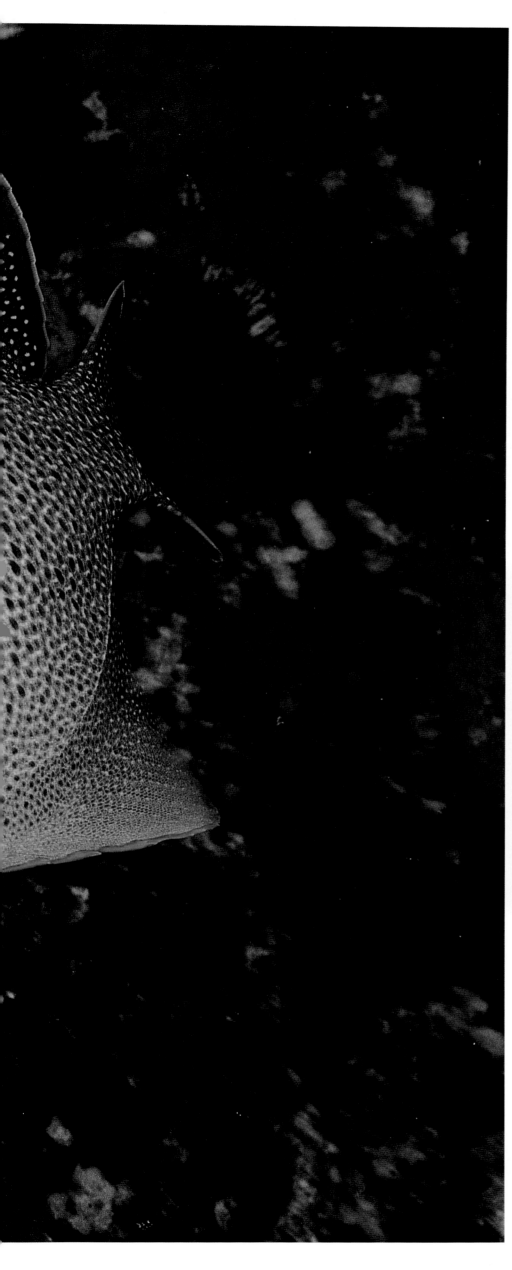

On them live an incredible quantity of pink, red and purple sea anemones, populated by curious clownfish and sometimes by magnificent porcelain crabs.

There are also long-legged red and yellow starfish and cushion stars, and especially huge sea urchins with their sharp spines. I've rested an arm, knee or leg on one during almost every dive, receiving a very painful but fortunately short-lived sting as just punishment for my carelessness. The pain

132-133 A magnificent angelfish *(Pomacanthus semicirculatus)*, with the characteristic pattern on the bottom of its snout, swims among the sponge-covered rocks of Sister Bank.

disappears in a few minutes, but traces of the spines remain visible under the skin for several days.

I made my first dive at Anse Marron Bank, on the southernmost tip of La Digue Island. On land, a splendid circle of rocks emerges from the sea and stretches along the beach into the greenery; in the sea, on a plateau no more than 25 metres deep are other rocks, lying next to one another, forming narrow passages with vertical walls rising to a height of 10-15 metres, mere clefts which are only just wide enough let a diver through, and sometimes insuperable.

133 An emperor angelfish *(Pomacanthus imperator)* flees from the diver in the waters off Félicité Rock. This angelfish usually lives alone, near rock formations.

134 This photo shows a pretty bivalve mollusc shell with zigzag edging. This inhabitant of the ocean is more likely to be found on the wrecks where it likes to grow than on reefs.

135 The terrible crown-of-thorns (*Acanthaster plancii*), the coral-eating starfish, is fortunately uncommon in the Seychelles. The spines of this echinoderm are highly poisonous, and can cause a very painful injury to careless divers.

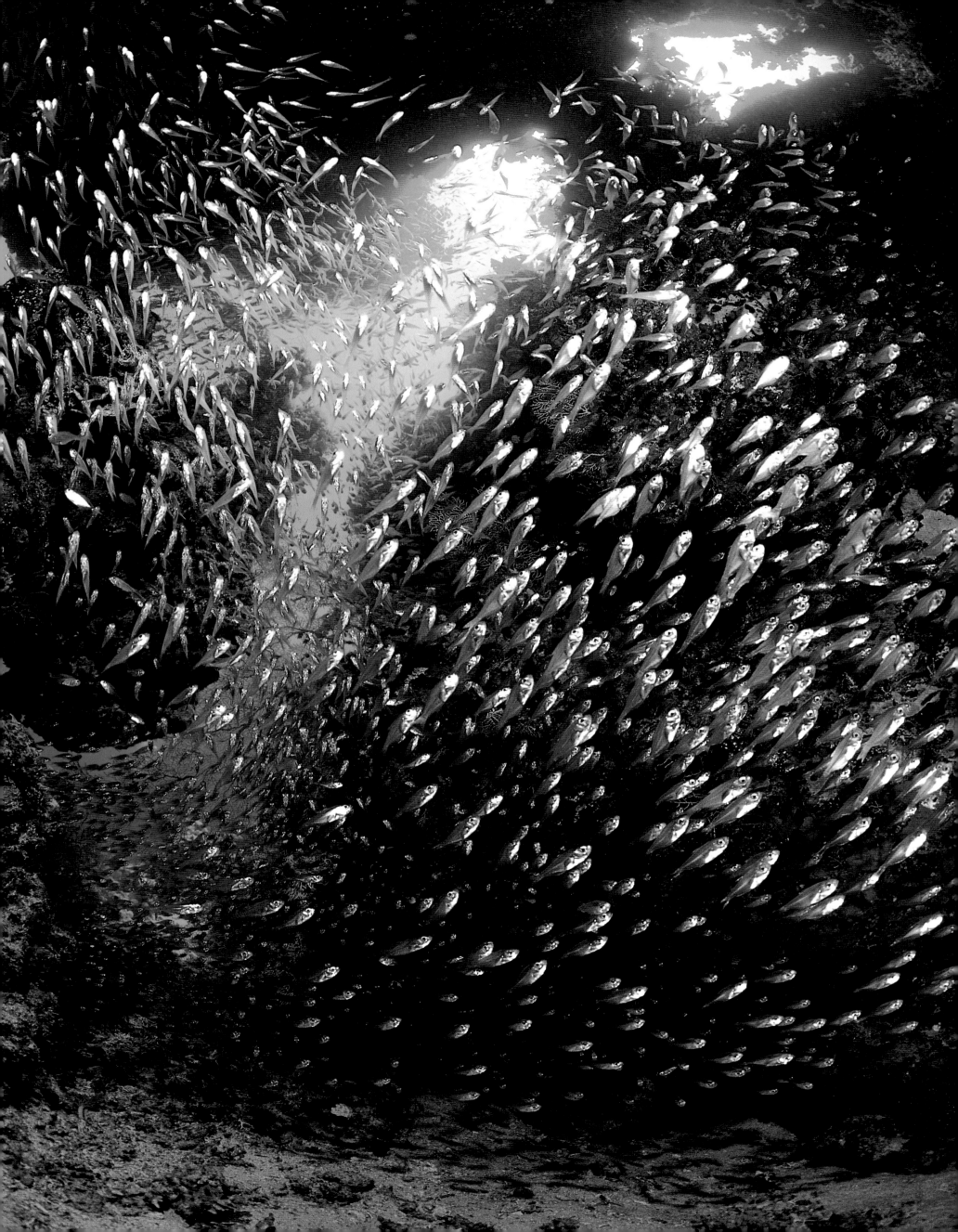

Shoals of tiny glassfish, another common sight on these dives, sometimes appear in the narrowest passages. Sometimes the current hits a passage broadside on, making it difficult to get through; you risk being battered against the rock and the ubiquitous sea urchins, and you may even find yourself face to face with a frightened small shark or disturb a big ray resting in a hollow slightly larger than the others, which swims off, folding back its wings or swimming nose-up to get through a narrow passage. Everywhere there are whitespotted soldierfish and different kinds of angelfish: the emperor angelfish *(Pomacanthus imperator)*, the royal angelfish *(Pygoplites diacanthus)* and the blue-edged angelfish *(Pomacanthus semicircolatus)*.

Diving off Sister Bank, around the islands that close the Praslin and La Digue group to the east, is very enjoyable. Here, the scenery is more varied: there are rocks covered with barnacle sponges and plateaux of coral sand, elkhorn coral formations and cracks inhabited by shoals of small fish. In a crevice between two rocks with pink and orange patches is a huge shoal of glassfish, undulating in the undertow. As I swim up the shoal parts, and the threatening snout of a huge moray eel appears right in the middle of the archway it forms. Last comes an attractive shoal of *Tra-*

chinotus bailloni, known as smallspotted pompano, though I call them the pompano with the buttoned jacket because they have four or five darker round spots just like buttons on the side, halfway up their splendid silver coats, in a straight line between the eye and the middle of the large sickle-shaped tail. Another great dive, one of the most attractive and varied, is at Brissare, a rock that emerges from the sea not far from the northern promontory of Mahé, near Praslin. I like to think that the name is a corruption of the word "bizarre". There's nothing bizarre about the rock itself – it's just one of many that suddenly stick up out of the sea on the Seychelles shelf – but the underwater scene is definitely bizarre and characteristic. On a plateau no more than 18 metres down, covered with seaweed, porcupine coral and branching fire coral, lie a number of great rocks like sleeping giants. Large batfish and dense shoals of parrotfish gather round them to feed, then dart off at an amazing speed.

136 In the waters off Trompeuse Rock there are numerous crevices and ravines among the granite rocks, often inhabited by thousands of glassfish *(Parapriacanthus sp.)*.

137 Félicité Rock resembles a minaret, which emerges from the surface of the sea from a depth of 20 metres. A shoal of soldierfish *(Myripristis murdjan)* can be seen following the current at its base, at the entrance to an open-ended grotto.

138-139 A majestic skate glides along the sandy ocean floor. It will probably cover itself with sand with a few quick flicks of its "wings", and lie in wait for an unwary victim.

If you swim up to the rock emerging from the sea, numerous groups of striped or Bengal snappers appear, and dense shoals of yellow-backed fusiliers dart by. Big moray eels peep out from their holes and you're quite likely to encounter a turtle busily munching seaweed or a scorpionfish (especially *Pterois radiata*) which moves lazily but pounces like lightning to capture its prey. Some 10 metres down there's a pretty open-ended grotto with a floor of white coral sand; if you venture into it, you'll find yourself out on the opposite side in a flash, forced through by the violent current that seems to concentrate at this point, but overtaken by a carangid that came in at the same time nevertheless.

Every so often it's a good idea to look up towards the surface; on the side where the tide beats against the rock, creating a huge undertow, you're sure to see at least one pair of shy eagle rays playing on the waves, as well as the occasional snipefish. The dive is not very deep, so you can easily swim all the way round the rock, even if you want to take your time over studying the details.

The Chimney Rocks dive, around another rock in the middle of the sea, far to the south of La Digue, is also unforgettable. Once again, not more than 25 metres down,

139 Some magnificent skate are commonly encountered during dives among the inner islands. The one shown in this photograph was perhaps disturbed by the photographer; however, it kept swimming around the place where it had been resting, as if it was waiting for me to go away.

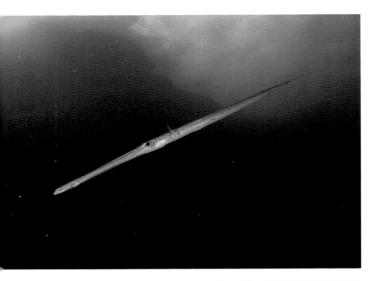

there's one of the loveliest, most vivid and flourishing coral gardens I've ever seen; a veritable aquarium containing many species of coral-dwelling fish, including numerous trunkfish of various kinds, puffers and squirrelfish. Above, where the sheer side of the rock forms a kind of horseshoe, a formation of over 10 eagle rays play in the waves; as usual they don't want to be approached, and swim off in different directions.

An even easier dive is at Channel Rocks, halfway between Praslin and La Digue. It's no deeper than 16 metres, quite well protected, and possible all year round. I've seen rocks covered with barnacle sponges of the brightest imaginable red, shoals of red and silver bream mingling together and dancing softly in the current, and a frightened turtle, perhaps upset because a murex with a huge shell has climbed onto its back to hitch a lift.

Then there are Trompeuse Rocks, more rocks in the middle of the sea with coloured crevices, whose shapes and colours recall those of the Mediterranean at Ventotene and Santo Stefano, except that here, they're sometimes occupied by shoals of glassfish, and Félicité Rock, another smooth rock, sharp towards the surface, with a grotto inhabited by a shoal of squirrelfish, its walls covered with yellow *Parazohantus*.

140 Brissare is one of the most densely inhabited diving sites in the inner islands. Trumpetfish *(Fistularia commersonii)* regularly swim among the waves near the surface (top), while dense shoals of silvery fish *(Lutjanus fulviflamma* and *Lutjanus quinquelineatus)* swim over the coral (bottom).

140-141 At Round Island, just a few metres down, a magnificent shoal of grey mullet *(Valamugil seheli)* drifts along, rocked by the continual motion of the waves.

142-143
The smallspotted pompano *(Trachinotus bailloni)* usually lives in lagoons and in the vicinity of quiet stretches of sand. Like the larger silver pompano it isn't shy and is easily approached, so some good photos can be taken.

Diving at Round Island, off the eastern promontory of Praslin, is different again. Here, the rocks are not embedded in the sand but merely rest on it, forming a series of holes, lairs and ravines. In addition to angelfish and trunkfish a few small sharks, fearful of unpleasant encounters, lurk there; above all there's an enormous number of cowries. Just under the surface of the water, shoals of grey mullet are commonly encountered; it's like being in a sort of tropical Mediterranean.

Another must is diving on the Ennerdale, in the middle of the channel between Mahé and Praslin. Here, an old cargo ship went down, bending and splitting in two as it sank. It lies on the sandy sea bed some 30 metres down, covered with seaweed. The wreck looks almost twisted; the bow points upwards and the sea creates a weird and dangerous play of currents on the deck side. If you're not careful, and get too close, you're liable to be shot towards the surface at a dangerously fast speed. Huge oysters with zigzag mouths and small sea fans cling to the twisted sheet metal, and the usual shoals of snappers swim through the middle. Big rays stop and rest in the shelter formed by the keel; if disturbed, they just swim a few metres away.

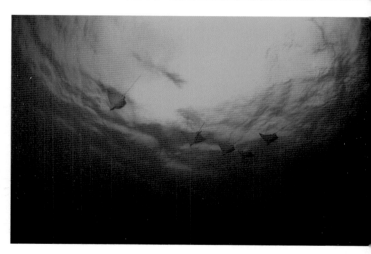

143 Eagle rays (*Aetobatus narinari*), alone or in formation, often ride the waves of the Seychelles. Sadly, these fish are very shy and quite hard to approach.

144-145 The Spanish dancer *(Hexabranchus sanguineus)* often lives in symbiosis with a magnificent shrimp *(Periclimenes imperator)*, which hides among the folds of its mantle, or in its lacy gill tuft. It is camouflaged so well that it often escapes even the closest scrutiny.

146 This unusual form of camouflage was observed in the waters off Channel Rocks; two lionfish *(Pterois antennata)* hide in the crevice of a rock covered with sponges of the same colour.

147 top The black-saddled toby *(Cantigaster valentini)* has weird social habits. It either lives alone or forms veritable harems; only rarely is it bound to a regular mate.

147 bottom Filefish, so called because of their rough skin, are very shy creatures, which spend much of their time motionless in their burrows.

I once dived with Teach at Islot, the rock situated a few hundred metres from the north headland of Mahé.

I'd fitted a macro lens, but it didn't seem like a very good decision; I saw some pretty white sea fans and an eagle ray much closer than usual, and swam through a lovely open-ended siphon with views that deserved a wide-angle lens.

Finally, under a coral, I glimpsed a big cuttlefish. I started taking photos.

I was beginning to think that I might as well use up the whole film on that subject when I felt Teach touch my arm, his eyes laughing behind his mask as he pointed something out. Teach is a Canadian sailor, a member of the *Fantasea*'s crew; he's a precise, totally reliable worker, a tough guy.

He has an unusual ability to follow divers' bubbles and pick them up in the dinghy when they emerge, even in the most tempestuous sea. Teach is nearly always serious; he rarely smiles, but has a lovely, boyish way of laughing with his eyes.

Now he was just laughing with his eyes, and pointing to the instrument panel of the oxygen cylinder. The instruments were OK, we weren't deep and we hadn't been diving long, so it took me a while to see what he was getting at.

148 The impressive granite rocks of Trompeuse are almost entirely covered with colourful sponges, particularly the bright red ones, and play host to numerous coral-dwelling fish.

149 This photo shows a granite rock face entirely colonised by some of the most spectacular life forms in the Seychelles, including sponges of various shapes and colours, and an impressive sea fan with its delicate branches.

150 Cowries can often be seen taking advantage of the darkness to scuttle among the grottoes of Round Island. This is a *Ciprea tigris*, so called because of the characteristic spots on its shell.

150-151 A large hermit crab *(Dardanus sp.)* has found a magnificent home in a triton shell.

There, attached to the instrument panel was a tiny creature, no more than an inch long, a little round ball with eight tiny tentacles and two clearly visible eyes, a cute, almost transparent little thing. The association of ideas was immediate. Of course it couldn't be the offspring of the cuttlefish we were photographing, but maybe it was a relative – perhaps a grandchild – or at least, that's what I like to think.

152-153 The wreck of the *Ennerdale* has been densely colonised over the years by large numbers of sea fans, soft corals and bivalve molluscs; numerous fish also swim among its planking.

Unusually, different species live together: snappers such as *Lutjanus bengalensis*, recognisable by the four yellow stripes on its back and its blue belly, and goggle-eye (*Priacanthus hamrur*).

154-155 Along the walls
of Sister Bank a shoal
of glassfish suddenly
parts to reveal the snout
of a giant moray

(Gymnothorax javanicus)
which has come out of
its burrow, its curiosity
perhaps aroused by the
diver's presence.

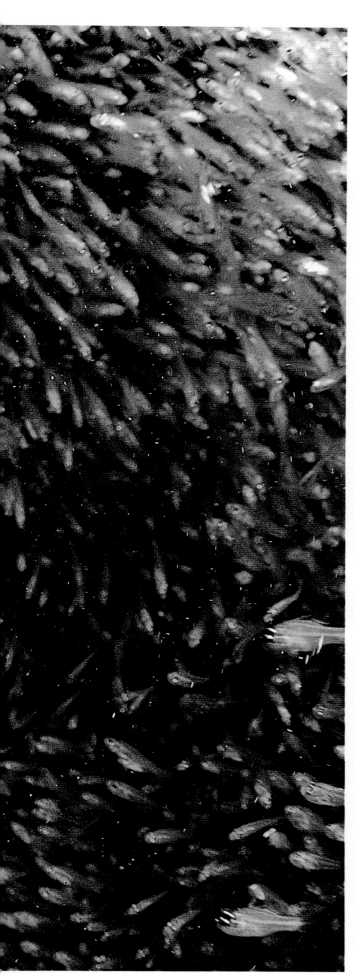

155 top This attractive cuttlefish, cleverly camouflaged to blend in with the surrounding environment, was spotted at Islot, a small rock off the northernmost tip of Mahé.

155 bottom This small grouper *(Epinephelus tauvina)* was so shy that it tried to hide from the camera by camouflaging itself among the seaweed.

156 Numerous crabs hide on a thick rope long abandoned in the sea, take refuge in an empty *Lambis* shell, or peep out from a crack between the corals.

156-157 A tiny cephalopod tries to camouflage itself on the control panel of Teach's breathing apparatus.

158-159 A veritable merry-go-round of snappers can sometimes be seen in the waters of Brissare. This photo shows a group of big-eye snappers *(Lutjanus lutjanus)*, which usually shoal in hundreds.

160 Young domino damselfish *(Dascyllus trimaculatus)* swim among the tentacles of a huge sea anemone.

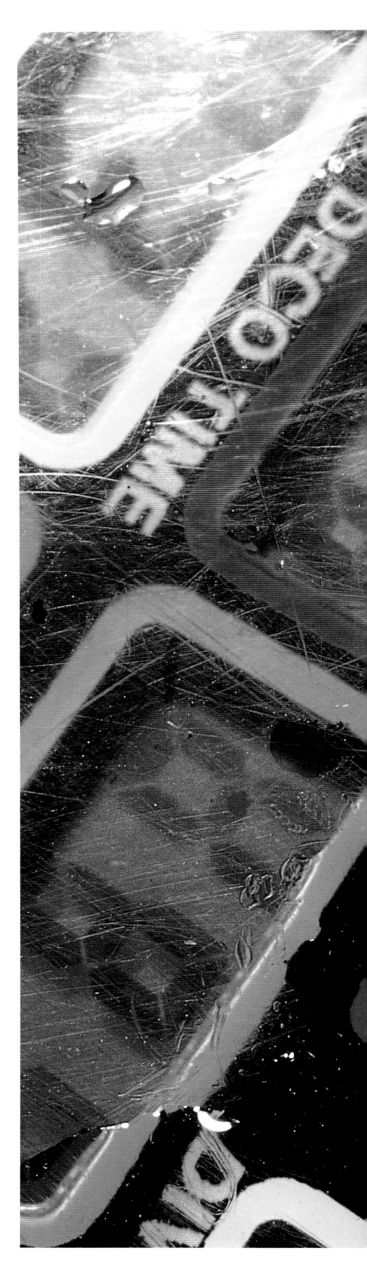